# THE BLACK MAN'S
# NORTH
# AND EAST AFRICA

# THE BLACK MAN'S NORTH AND EAST AFRICA

YOSEF ben-JOCHANNAN
and GEORGE E. SIMMONDS

Black Classic Press
Baltimore

# THE BLACK MAN'S NORTH AND EAST AFRICA

Copyright 1971
Yosef ben-Jochannan and George E. Simmonds
First published by Alkebu-lan Book Associates

Published 2005
by Black Classic Press

All Rights Reserved.

Library of Congress Card Catalog Number: 2004117966
ISBN 10: 1-57478-032-8
ISBN 13: 978-1-57478-032-1

Cover art by Michelle D. Wright, rendered from
the original cover by Yosef ben-Jochannan

Printed by BCP Digital
An affiliate company of Black Classic Press

Founded in 1978, Black Classic Press specializes in bringing to light obscure and significant works by and about people of African descent. If our books are not available in your area, ask your local bookseller to order them.

You can purchase books and obtain a list of our titles from:

Black Classic Press
c/o List
P.O. Box 13414
Baltimore, MD 21203
also visit:
www.blackclassic.com

Alkebu-lan Foundation, Inc. Heritage Series

THE BLACK MAN'S NORTH and EAST

AFRICA

by

Yosef ben-Jochannan

Instructor of History: Marymount College,
Tarrytown, New York.
Adjunct. Assoc. Prof. of History: Pace
College, New York City, New York.
Adjunct Prof. of History: University of
the City of New York, Borough of Man-
hattan Community College, N.Y., N.Y.

and

George E. Simmonds

Instructor of African, African-American &
African-Caribbean History and Culture:
Harlem Preparatory School Of New York,
Inc., New York City, New York.

I HAVE SHOWN IN THE PRECEDING PAGES THAT RELIGION
HAD ALREADY BEEN DEVELOPED IN THE PIGMY, AND FURTHER
IN THIS WORK I HAVE EXPLAINED THE MEANING AND ORIGIN
OF MAGIC.

IF DR. FRAZER WILL READ THIS, HE WILL PREHAPS MO-
DIFY THE OPINIONS HE HAS EXPRESSED IN RECENT WORKS,
AND THUS PREVENT THE DISSEMINATION OF FALSE IDEAS DUE
TO IGNORANCE OF THE FUNDAMENTAL PRINCIPLES UNDERLYING
TOTEMISM, SIGN LANGUAGE, MYTHOLOGY, AND THE RITUAL OF
EGYPT.

NO OBJECTION CAN POSSIBLY BE RAISED TO ANY MAN, OR
WOMAN, HOLDING SUCH PRIVATE OPINIONS AS THEY CHOOSE,
BUT THERE IS A VERY GREAT OBJECTION TO MEN, OCCUPYING
THE POSITIONS OF TEACHERS OR PROFESSORS, DISSEMINAT-
ING EXPLODED, ANTIQUATED, AND WRONG IDEAS WHICH SCIEN-
TIFIC RESEARCH AND MATERIAL EVIDENCE PROVED TO BE FALSE.

(From Albert Churchward, M.
D., M.R.C.P., F.G.S., etc.,
ORIGIN & EVOLUTION OF THE HU-
MAN RACE, London: George Al-
len & Unwin Ltd., 1921)

The above citation expresses the position of the contents of this book.

CONTENTS

ABBREVIATIONS, PHRASES, ETC.

C.E. = Christian Era = A.D. = After the Death of Jesus Christ

B.C.E. = Before the Christian Era = B.C. = Before the Birth of Jesus Christ

*From* The Penitential Tyrant; or, Slave Trader Reformed, *Thomas Branagan, New York, 1807. Princeton University Library.*

ILLUSTRATIONS:

INTRODUCTORY REMARKS

I call this aspect of our excursion into the RACIST attempts by people who call themselves "SEMITES, CAUCASIANS, LIBERALS," and the likes - including "NEW LEFT" and "NEW RIGHT," an "INTRODUCTION." But, in reality, it is neither that nor a GUIDE. The constant attempts by the "LIBERAL RESPONSIBLE LEADER-SHIP" of "WELL-MEANING WHITE LIBERALS," and equally "WELL-MEANING INTEGRATED NEGROES," have shown to all thinking BLACK PEOPLE throughout the world that unless we establish our own values of "RIGHT" and "WRONG," and take every means at our disposal to "RIGHT" "WRONGS" committed against us, we will never survive the impending GENOCIDE (culturally and physically) planned for us by those farthest to the "RIGHT" and AIDED and ABETTED by those nearest and far-thest to the "LEFT." For in this ravaging of the BLACKS, culturally, starting with the placing of us in biblical history and theology as DEVILS and the PERSONS most-responsible for our own enslavement by our slavemasters, which still goes on in different degrees in different lands - including our "MOTHER AFRICA," we must realize that "WHITE AMERICA" (Jewish, Christian, Leftist, Rightist, or otherwise) still sees the African and his descendants as they were one hundred (100) years before "President Abraham Lincoln's EMANCIPATION PROCLAMATION." If there be any doubt of this, the following extract from the speech of the United States of America's Representative to the United Nations Organization, the late Adlai Stevenson - Ambassador and Minister Plenipotentiary, with respect to his country's attempt to support Belgian imperialism and colonialism in the Republic of the Congo (Leopoldville, correctly KINSHASA), and to protect "WHITES" who were engaged for generations in the "systematic planned genocide" against the Congolese people under the pretext of "...BRINGING CHRISTIANITY AND CIVILIZATION TO THE NATIVES..." [many of them in the service of American "FREE ENTERPRISE" engaged in profit-making from the LIFE-BLOOD and DEATH (Genocide) of the Congolese people], must be read and compared to that which was stated in answer to him by the Foreign Minister of Congo (Brazzaville) Honourable Charles Gannao. Stevenson's speech, in part:

> The grim story of thousands of innocent civilians - many of
> them foreign-illegally seized, brutalized, and threatened,

and many murdered by rebels against the Congo government....
Every means-legal, moral, and humane, including the United
Nations - was exhausted to protect their lives and secure
their release - all without avail. When it became apparent
that there was no hope, the Belgian and American governments,
with the cooperation of the Government of the United Kingdom,
and with the express authorization of the sovereign government
of the Democratic Republic of the Congo, undertook an emergency
rescue mission to save the lives of these innocent people.
The operation was carried out with restraint, courage, discipline, and dispatch.

What Stevenson failed to mention throughout his entire speech was that

the so-called "DEMOCRATIC REPUBLIC OF THE CONGO," at that time, was the

creation of the same colonalists and imperialists who were responsible for the

murder of the leader of the original and only true "DEMOCRATIC GOVERNMENT"

elected by the African people of Congo - the late Honourable Patrice Lumumba.

Gannao's reply, in part, to Stevenson's speech:

What humanitarian principles are at stake, when, on the pretext
of saving lives of an insignificant number of whites, tens of
thousands of blacks are massacred - innocent blacks who know
nothing of political maneuvers and whose only crime is that of
having been born in a country whose natural resources are shock-
ingly plentiful?... The Stanleyville aggression is an extremely
serious matter. It has proved, in striking fashion, that there
is no place for the black man in this world wherever he may be,
whether it be in a country to which he came in the same way as
others before him, or in his own homeland of Africa. Indeed, it
is sufficient for a minority of white imperialists and racists
to appear anywhere, for the black man to find himself deprived
of every right, even the right to live. Now, even in his own
country, even in a country with a black Government, the black
man no longer feels safe.

Strangely enough Stevenson's speech before the United Nations Security Council

was published by THE NEW YORK TIMES of December 14, 1964. The rebuttal by

Gannao, on the otherhand, had to be extracted from the same Security Council

Official Records, 1170, of December 9, 1964, pages 14 through 16. Obviously

the New York Times slogan, that "...ONLY NEWS THAT'S FIT TO PRINT..," did not

apply to Gannao's speech; but it most certainly did with respect to the "WHITE

LIBERAL" stance of the representative of the government which have BLACK

(Congolese) PEOPLE'S of Africa interest at heart; but of course no interest

for those who shared the same common "CITIZENSHIP" with Stevenson. This is quite

in keeping with "TRUE LIBERALISM," one would imagine, why Gannao's speech was

not treated in the TIMES as that by the "WHITE LIBERAL" whom millions of

BLACK Americans one time voted to become President of the United States of

America.

It would have been sufficient to show that the same attitudes of White
CAUCASIAN or SEMITIC America towards BLACKS (so-called "NEGROES") of North and
East Africa is typical in many respects to BLACKS all over the entire continent of Alkebu-lan (Africa). But TIME of December 4, 1964 brought forward
the true meaning for the aggression against the Congolese people by the
combined "WHITE" governments engaged in the aggression against the Congo, and
their "AFRICAN CHRISTIAN" subservients they had forced upon the Congolese
people, for their own economic gains. But the article also capitalized on the
death of a so-called "AMERICAN CHRISTIAN MISSIONARY," Dr. Carlson, who had
failed to notice that his version of "CHRISTIANITY" was much more needed in
the United States of America than in Africa - where it began in Egypt and
Ethiopia. Thus the late doctor's fellow colonialist-minded TIME's commentator
or commentators claimed that he was murdered by the hands of:

    ...A RABBLE OF DAZED, IGNORANT NATIVES....

The above remarks from one of the United States of America's "responsible"
communication machine only adds to the proof of the true nature of "WHITE"
non-racism under "BLACK" pressure. But the TIME'S article went on to say that:

> ...Black African civilization - with its elaborate trappings
> of half a hundred sovereignties, governments, and U.N. dele-
> gations is largely a pretense...," etc..

The protectors of WHITE RACISM, the TIME, wondered further with its own
apparent type of contempt for BLACK PEOPLE, including those of the so-called
"NEGRO-WHITE LIBERAL COALITION:"

> ...whether Black Africa can be taken seriously at all, or
> whether, for the forseeable future, it is beyond the reach
> of reason.

The two citations made, with respect to the TIME'S article, appeared in a
very well noted medium which most "WHITE LIBERALS" would call non-RACIST. But
one should easily observe the opposite. Further, it is obvious that the writer,
or writers of this article, carefully failed to mention that the African people
had nothing whatsoever to do with the making of the "...HUNDRED SOVEREIGNTIES"
mentioned. That, instead, they were created by Europeans and European-Americans
(the type Ambassador Adlai Stevenson defended) at the BERLIN and BRUSSELS

conferences of the latter part of the 19th century C.E. (1884-1896). These were
the colonalists and "Christian Missionaries" who "PARTITIONED" the African's
continent in the JIGSAW PUZZLE the article so contemptuously criticized. It is
incongruent to expect that the TIME, or anyother major European-American representative of foreign capital investors and "Christian"Missionaries (which
have greatly enriched their treasuries with the proceeds of the BLACK MAN'S
labor from the days of his enslavement by Europeans and European-Americans),
would have failed to act in the same manner consistent among many WHITE
Christian and Jewish RACISTS who have claimed that NORTH and EAST-African
history and culture are of their indigenous heritage. The TIME'S article,
in this case, being no less RACIST than the statements by "educators" who
claimed that their North and East African heritage were free of "BLACK AFRICANS"
(the so-called "NEGROES" invented by the "DISCOVERERS OF AFRICA"). The
"...IGNORANT SAVAGES..." the TIME referred to is nothing new; this being
common in the teachings of the Jewish HOLY TORAH and the Christian HOLY BIBLE
with respect to all of the non-"CHOSEN." Of course,I mean the many versions
of the TORAH and BIBLE as plagiarized to make JEHOVAH  and JESUS CHRIST "White
Caucasian-Semites" from the GARDEN OF EDEN. The same "Garden of Eden," in this
case, is the place where there was never a BLACK MAN or WOMAN. Why? Because
Jehovah (including the TRINITY - Father, Son, and Holy Ghost) allegedly created
the first "Negro" or "Black Man" when he sanctioned the "CURSE" Noah (Noe)
placed upon "THE CHILDREN OF CHANNAN" (Canaan; Ham's son; Noah's grandson;
Adam and Eve's descendants).

This INTRODUCTION,  which follows no previous criteria of established
"SCHOLARSHIP" or "ACADEMIC" priorities by those who now call themselves
"AFRICANISTS" or "WHITE LIBERAL AFRICAN HISTORIANS," and even "EGYPTOLOGISTS,"
attempts to lead the reader to documented information relative to the basic
cause why there could have been the type of disguised RACISM and RELIGIOUS
BIGOTRY in the speech of Ambassador Stevenson; equally the comments of the
writer or writers of the article in the TIME  . But, what is the cause for all
of these RACIST proclamations? It all began with the claim of a "GOD'S CHOSEN
PEOPLE" myth in the Hebrew ("Jewish") HOLY TORAH, which was compounded by the

Christian HOLY BIBLE additions to justify European and European-American -
WHITE (Caucasian and Semitic) teaching about their own "RACIAL SUPERIORITY."
This conclusion can be clearly understood when one examines the following
map* and compares it with the others on pages 18 , 42 , and 65 of this book.
It is taken from a book, ARAB WORLD NEW AFRICA, published by W. H. Sadlier,
New York, 1968, which is being used as a high school text on Africa.

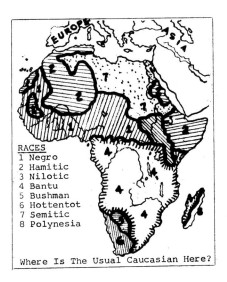

RACES
1 Negro
2 Hamitic
3 Nilotic
4 Bantu
5 Bushman
6 Hottentot
7 Semitic
8 Polynesia

Where Is The Usual Caucasian Here?

The above map is typical of the type of SEMITIC and HAMITIC syndromes
which modern professors have constantly engaged in, and of which I have been
describing in my previous works; all of which I have more closely detailed in
this book. It is commonly shown in at least 70% of all books I have seen
dealing with the subjects of ETHNOGRAPHY and ANTHROPOLOGY of African peoples
the world over. This type of publication is generally the sole responsibility
of the "EDUCATOR" that developed it, and not so much the publisher; the latter
generally being unaware of the documentary evidence behind what they publish.

*This map was originally in colors. It has been cross-hatched and dotted in
different patterns for your convenience. It was necessary to make it BLACK
and WHITE in order to keep the cost of reproduction at a low level. Follow the
HEAVY OUTLINES and NUMBERS within them for identification of the "RACIAL
GROUPS" of Africa À-LA-RACISM. You probably would be surprised to know that
there are at least FIVE (5) more RACES ascribed to Africa by modern "EDUCATORS"
who are acclaimed "AUTHORITIES ON AFRICA" and on "BLACK STUDIES" - the so-
called "AFRICANISTS."

Any attempt by an African, or any person of African origin, to write
Africa's history according to so-called "ACADEMIC DISCIPLINE," as established
by European and European-American "EDUCATORS" or "AUTHORITIES ON AFRICA"
(à-la-Western style), is tantamount to removing the African slaves as property
of their European and/or European-American masters, without seriously damaging
their economic interest. For at no time will the White slave masters, nor the
children of the White slave masters, write of their Black slaves as their
equal. This also holds true for the ex-slaves and the ex-slaves' children.

The above statement becomes much more apparent with respect to its
BLACK-WHITE realities, as one considers that it is the INTERPRETATION OF
HISTORY which makes the difference between what is "RIGHT" or "WRONG," "GODLY"
or "UN-GODLY," "MORAL" or "IMMORAL." This citation is a crucial factor in the
title of the colonial imperialist Henry Morton Stanley's book, DARKEST AFRICA.
It is equally applicable to all of the European and European-American so-called
"CHRISTIAN MISSIONARIES" propaganda about African religions that were developed
hundreds of years before they arrived at their "EUROPEANIZED VERSION" of
North-African Christianity. For example: European and European-American
"CHRISTIAN MISSIONARIES" constantly complain that "...AFRICANS WORSHIP PAGAN
GODS; AFRICANS ARE IDOLATERS; AFRICANS ARE UNCIVILIZED;" etc. The fact is that
any GOD is a "PAGAN" to any person who does not believe in IT or HIM, but in
another. Christians are "PAGANS" for Jews; and Jews are equally "PAGANS" in
the eyes of Christians; etc. This form of RELIGIOUS BIGOTRY is best perpetuated
through religious education in parochial schools (and Sunday schools) in
churches, synagogues and mosques throughout the United States of America under
the disguise of "...THE AMERICAN WAY OF LIFE." These institutions generally
perpetuate the type of BRAINWASHING that eventually becomes RACISM and RELIGIOUS
BIGOTRY; this being best demonstrated in the "CHOSEN PEOPLE" myth prevalent
in Judaeo-Christian theology. This is part and parcel of the religious doctrines
that created a "HELL" and "HEAVEN" mystery system to frighten those who dared
to differ with the teachings of how "CREATION" took place under a Jewish GOD
called "JEHOVAH." Anyother GOD,... including the other so-called "SEMITE" by

the name of "JESUS CHRIST," is taught by most "GOD-FEARING AMERICANS" to be a "FALSE GOD." Of course most Jews, of any color, consider their fellow Jew — JESUS CHRIST - an "IMPOSTER" and a "FALSE GOD." But who is to say which "GOD" is "FALSE" or "TRUE"? There is a sort of GENTLEMEN'S AGREEMENT on this point between European and European-American JEWS and CHRISTIANS with respect to their EUROPEANIZED and EURO-AMERICANIZED versions of Judaism and Christianity; but none whatsoever with respect to any and all African religions that are not considered of African origin, which of course includes Judaism that had its birth in the bosom of an African named MOSES in Africa - Egypt.* Because of this type of PROPAGANDA, there is no real examination of religion permitted; thus no truly OPEN SCRUTINY of the FALSEHOOD or TRUTHFULLNESS of the corruptive indoctrination of the established religious myths laid down by certain men who can, allegedly, verify that "...THE HOLY BIBLE..." (the "OLD" and "NEW" Testament) "...WAS WRITTEN BY GOD-INSPIRED MEN." The major assumption here is that all of the other books and writings by other men of non-SEMITIC or non-CAUCASIAN origin were not "GOD-INSPIRED WRITINGS;" thus the only "TRUE GOD" becomes a "WHITE" one with a "SEMITIC" NOSE.

Supposedly, I am not being very "ACADEMIC" when I cite the type of RACISM and RELIGIOUS BIGOTRY being perpetuated by men and women who refer to themselves by such names as "RABBI, REVEREND, MINISTER, PRIEST, IMAN," and the likes of same; this being TRUE even for those who do the same under the disguise of "ACADEMIC SCHOLARSHIP" as they perpetuate their "SEMITIC NORTH AFRICA" syndrome and RACIST CAUCASIANISM for the same area of Africa. This, they are doing in order to exclude a certain segment of African PEOPLE they call "NEGROES" (among many other degrading names they have invented for them) from North Africa's indigenous history and High-Culture (civilization). It is not different from what was done with respect to their "HAMITIC EAST AFRICA" syndrome. All of this stem from the so-called "INDO-EUROPEAN ARYAN" and "SEMITIC" peoples need for a connection to Africa's antiquity - to the proven "GARDEN OF EDEN." Of course both "SEMITES" and "HAMITES" have become of recent "CAUCASIANS," or at least "CAUCASOIDS;" thus <u>Jesus Christ, Jehovah, Moses,</u>

---

*Kimit originally, according to the indigenous BLACK PEOPLE of the continent they called "ALKEBU-LAN - which the Greeks and Romans misnamed "AFRICA."

Mohamet ibn Abdullah, Al'lah, and all of the "...PEOPLE OF THE BOOK" (from a White RACIST point of view), are now promoted to the Kosher Rank of "CAU-CASIANS" and/or "SEMITES." This too, is due to the need of the so-called "SEMITES" to be accepted into the RANKS of their former persecutors in Europe and those of European-America; all of this being attributable to the many so-called "ACADEMICIANS" and "SCHOLARS" who are also engaged in writing most of the materials used in "AFRICAN" and "BLACK" Studies Courses throughout the United States of America's institutions of higher learning.

Should people of African origin have to continue compromising themselves to writings that profess a "SEMITIC JEHOVAH" and/or "JESUS CHRIST," or even a "HAMITIC AL'LAH," as "...THE ONE AND ONLY TRUE GOD..."? No. Africans should be fully aware of the fact that "I AM" - the GOD RA..." of the Nile Valleys (Blue and White) and the Great Lakes regions of Alkebu-lan (Africa) predated all three of the other GODS mentioned before by thousands of years. Why should African-Americans ignore that their indigenous African ancestors of Egypt's BOOK OF THE DEAD, written about c. 4100 B.C.E., preceded the birth of the first Hebrew (misnomered "JEW") - Abraham - by at least 2470 years; and at least 2902 years before another fellow African named Moses (the African who brought forward the "ADAM AND EVE IN THE GARDEN OF EDEN" theory and myth; also the "TEN COMMANDMENTS" which he plagiarized from the "NEGATIVE CONFESSIONS" of the "OSIRIAN DRAMA" of his Egyptian brethren,while he read the COFFIN TEXT, before he placed them into what is today called "THE FIVE BOOKS OF MOSES" or THE HOLY TORAH)? European-American ACADEMICS, "White Studies" if you please, have demanded that such be done. But, whose standard requirements are they? Are they the dictates established by indigenous Africans, or by persons directly descended from people of African ancestry, who recognize themselves as such, and with respect for said heritage and origin? Are they not by "ACADEMICIANS" whose interest a "CAUCASIAN, HAMITIC," or "SEMITIC" North Africa serve? Certainly the latter is the case.

It is precisely due to the "CAUCASIAN, HAMITIC" and "SEMITIC NORTH AFRICA" syndrome so prevalent amongst what is today called "AFRICANISTS, AUTHORITIES ON AFRICA, EGYPTOLOGISTS," and others of such ilk in the so-called class of "ACADEMICIANS" and "SCHOLARS," that I have decided to republish this very-much-revised book I wrote sometime ago and published in Puerto Rico during 1942 C.E. in one of the then "INDEPENDENT POLITICAL JOURNALS" for college students; this being at a time when I could not possibly convince one JET-BLACK Puerto Rican that the Moors of Spain were "LIGHT-SKINNED," muchless "DARK-SKINNED," worse yet "BLACK-SKINNED", Africans from the northwestern region of Africa. In Puerto Rico, at that period in history, at least 99.9% of the so-called "NATIVE POPULATION" was totally an amalgamation of the indigenous peoples Cristobal Colon (Christopher Columbus) called "CARIBS," indigenous African descendants called "MOROS" (Moors) and many from other parts of the African continent, and Europeans mostly from Spain; the latter two groups having arrived there for the first time (according to European and European-American writers) with Colon and his captain of the Santa Maria - Pietro Olonzo Niño[1] (an African Moor) in 1492 C.E.

There is enough written about the indigenous Africans - the so-called "NEGROES" or "AFRICANS SOUTH OF THE SAHARA," and THINGS AFRICAN, to satisfy anyone's hunger for learning about this topic. But, of late, how much of what has been written expresses any viewpoint of the indigenous Africans in the interpretations of their history and heritage by the so-called "AFRICANISTS," "EGYPTOLOGISTS" and others of different disciplines related and unrelated to Africa and her peoples? Practically nothing of late - the 19th and 20th century C.E. However, now that the indigenous Africans and others of African descent are again in position to write and teach about themselves, and of others too (including the former slavemasters and their offsprings), the Africans' side of history will again be heard from a BLACK PERSPECTIVE (interpretation); re-gardless of who wants to hear or read about it. Why? Because Africans should not have to prattle PERVERTED and PROSTITUTED versions of a "DISTORTED HISTORY" about themselves as written by so-called "WESTERN HISTORIANS, PALEONTOLOGISTS, ARCHAEOLOGISTS, ANTHROPOLOGISTS," and others of related and unrelated dis-ciplines - the so-called "WHITE LIBERAL AFRICANISTS." There is no justifiable reason whatsoever. As such; why should the perpetrators of the BIG LIE - the DISTORTERS of North Africa, Nile Valleys (Blue and White), and East Africa history and High-Culture - not be specifically identified along with CITATIONS from their RACIST and RELIGIOUSLY BIGOTED writings, maps, and other works they have used in their attempt to commit CULTURAL GENOCIDE against North and East Africa's indigenous sons and daughters, also against the descendants of said Africans who have been forced against their will to leave Africa and migrate to the "AMERICAS" as slaves around 1503 C.E.? There is none to withstand the bit of scrutiny that would not reveal a kind of a "GENTLEMAN'S AGREEMENT" between the so-called "SEMITIC" and "CAUCASIAN" academicians, historians, and other "EDUCATORS" in general; most of whom hide behind said titles and cloaks of respectability to give the impression of their alleged "UNBIAS ACADEMIC SCHOLARSHIP." Thus it is because of this reason, and many more stated before in most of my other works, that I have dedicated myself once more to the task of bringing to you (my students and the reading public at large), those who have bismirched, plagiarized, corrupted, and bastardized each and every aspect of Africa's (ALKEBU-LAN'S) ancient and current High-Cultures (civilizations) and Heritage - particularly that of North and East Africa.

It is not enough for African people at home in the continent, those gone abroad, and those born and living abroad, to write about themselves and their "MOTHER-LAND" - Alkebu-lan.[2] It is much more important that they correct the willful LIES, DISTORTIONS, HALF-TRUTHS and other FALSIFICATIONS and PLAGIAR-IZATIONS exemplified in the "TARZAN AND JANE" moving pictures and the European and European-American style "CHRISTIAN MISSIONARIES" con-man stories about the "...CANNIBAL AND HEATHEN AFRICANS WHO WERE UNCIVILIZED BEFORE THE ARRIVAL OF THE CHRISTIAN MISSIONARIES IN AFRICA." Such stories they created for the purpose of RAISING VERY LARGE SUMS OF MONEY under the pretext of "...BRINGING JESUS CHRIST TO THE HEATHEN NATIVES...'! All of said LIES are designed to give Europeans and European-Americans and their "NEGRO CONVERTS" a sense of SUPERIORITY over their so-called "...PAGAN AND HEATHEN NATIVES." The SHAKE-DOWN RACKET of "BRINGING CHRISTIANITY AND CIVILIZATION TO THE HEATHEN NATIVES" is as big a LIE as the fallacy of teaching that ... "SEMITIC PEOPLES WERE THE INDIGENOUS INHABITANTS OF NORTH AFRICA BEFORE, AND DURING, THE REIGN OF THE DYNASTIC PHARAOHS;" when history showed that "ETHIOPIANS"[3] with their:

...THICK LIPS, BROAD NOSE, WOOLLY HAIR, AND BURNT SKIN...,
etc. ruled all over ALKEBU-LAN (Africa), North and East included, before and
after the arrival of the first so-called "SEMITIC PEOPLES" from Asia - the
HYKSOS from the river banks of the Oxus about c. 1675 B.C.E.

This concentrated SAFARI (excursion) into the African-American (Black
Man, Ethiopian, "Negro," etc.) ancestors' history and heritage of NORTH and
EAST Africa is of the gravest importance. WHY? Because it is precisely within
these two geographic areas of Africa (ALKEBU-LAN) that European and European-
American (CAUCASIAN, SEMITE, HAMITE, or whatever-else) ACADEMICIANS, HISTORIANS,
and others, have found it necessary to lay claim in order to have an ancestral
origin beyond their oldest EUROPEAN ANCESTOR - Neanderthal Man - who dates
back only 300,000 years ago. For without said African ancestral heritage in
their origin, which goes back to Africa's Zinjanthropus boisie of c. 1,750,000
years, even in the case of the most ancient of their so-called "WHITE CAU-
CASIAN INDO-EUROPEAN ARYAN RACE" - the Greeks and Romans, they would have had
to be shown as the descendants of indigenous Ethiopians' (or Africans') ancestors
of "NEGROES" and "AFRICANS SOUTH OF THE SAHARA," even "BANTUS," of Kimit
(Egypt), Colchis (much of modern Turkey and areas in Europe around it), and
present-day Ethiopia (Itiopi or Kush); of whom Herodotus, Eusebius, Polybius
(and other Europeans and Asians of antiquity) described in the manner I have
already quoted at the bottom of page xii of this work.

Strangely enough, as we examine the pages of ancient history for any
justification to the most modern myth of "SEMITIC NORTH AFRICANS" and "HAMITIC
EAST AFRICANS" who were allegedly "the first to inhabit said regions of Africa,"
we are going to find that those who are perpetuating this MYTH are the same
people who owe more to their "NEGRO" origin and  heritage than anyone-else.
It is like those "NEGROES" who are "PASSING FOR WHITE" in the United States
of America having to prove their CAUCASIANESS beyond the point of those who
are accepted at birth as of "INDO-EUROPEAN ARYAN" or "WHITE ANGLO-SAXON
PROTESTANT CHRISTIAN" stock. But the "SEMITISTS" have quite another goal,
apparently. Unlike the "NEGROES" who are "PASSING FOR WHITE;" they are already
of European origin, thus they can better protect themselves from another

holocaust like that which Adolph Hitler initiated against their next of kin in the latter part of 1938 C.E. In this case, by creating a "SEMITIC NORTH AFRICAN ORIGIN" from whence the <u>ancestors of the Europeans</u> - Greeks - derived their basic values in every discipline of their High-Culture, including what has become "GREEK PHILOSOPHY," the "SEMITISTS" can also claim that they are in fact THE ORIGINAL INDIGENOUS ETHIOPIANS (Africans or "Negroes") OF EGYPT FROM WHOM ALL OF THE EUROPEANS ORIGINATED CULTURALLY, at least, if not RACIALLY. The victim, of course, as in all other cases in the plagiarization of Africa's prehistory, history and heritage, by Europeans and European-Americans (and a few "Negroes "),are the AFRICANS, AFRICAN-AMERICANS and AFRICAN-CARIBBEANS - those of US who are extremely PROUD OF OUR AFRICAN HERITAGE AND EXPERIENCE, OUR BLACKNESS never to be excluded. WHY? Because we have followed our indigenous African ancestors warning they wrote on the walls of their HOUSES OF THE GODS - Pyramids:

MAN (Africans) KNOW THYSELF.....KNOW THYSELF.

(by yosef ben-jochannan: September 1971)

THIS WORK IS DEDICATED TO THE HONOUR OF THE COUNTLESS AFRICAN PEOPLE, LIKE MYSELF, WHO SPENT DAYS, WEEKS, MONTHS, AND YEARS AT THE CORNERS OF 125th STREET AND 7th AVENUE ("Harlem" or "Marcus Garvey Square") LISTEN-ING TO THE MANY AFRICAN NATIONALIST ORATORS WHO TAUGHT THE MALCOM X's, STOKELY CARMICHAELs, ROY INNIS,' LEORY JONES,' AND MOST OF THE OTHER SO-CALLED "black nation-alists",THAT EVENTUALLY MADE THE WHITE NEWS MEDIA. FOR IT IS TO THESE "UNKNOWN BLACKS," WHO HELD STEADFASTLY TO THE TEACHINGS IN THE "PHILOSOPHY AND OPINIONS" OF THE LATE HONOURABLE MARCUS M. GARVEY ("the greatest of the BACK TO AFRICA MOVEMENT leaders"), THAT MOST OF THE CREDIT FOR THE CURRENT "BLACK REVOLUTION" IN PROGRESS THROUGHOUT THE UNITED STATES OF AMERICA MUST BE GIVEN. TO THEM, I REPEAT WHAT DR. EDWARD W. BLYDEN, LATE PRE-SIDENT OF THE COLLEGE OF LIBERIA, AND THE LATE HONOUR-ABLE PRESIDENT-GENERAL OF THE U.N.I.A., MARCUS M. GARVEY, SO PROUDLY REMINDED US:

Africa For The Africans,* Those At Home, And Those Abroad....**

- and -

The Africans Right To Be Wrong Is Sacred

---

*From Dr. Blyden's INAUGURAL ADDRESS as President of the College of Liberia, West Africa, c. 1883.
**Extension of Dr. Blyden's citation by Honourable Marcus M. Garvey.

SPECIAL CREDIT

   The end result of any book is what both reader and author anticipate with
great hope. But in the accomplishment of this achievement, it is those behind
the scene who are to be given special credit for the failure or success of the
"END RESULT." This book is no exception to this general rule; nor the people
who worked "BEHIND THE SCENE." To these people: Mrs. Marlene Maisonet, for
being able to decipher the various inserts and other handwritten notes related
to the original draft of the manuscript, and still turn out the splendid type-
written result she has; Miss Bess R. Terry, for her endless and almost-tire-
less editing and re-editing of the original handwritten manuscript, also the
final drafts and completed work; Mr. Carl Kalnek, for the meticulous manner
in which he checked each and every data related to the documentary evidence
of the facts presented, also the cited bibliography and its supplement; Miss
Barbara Renick of Multi-Print, Inc. (my printer) for her usual understanding
in making the END RESULT (from the printer's view) fit our very meager
financial budget; and to my daughter Collette Denise Makeda for her efforts in
aiding us with the selection of the many pictures used in the book; we owe a
SPECIAL DEBT OF GRATITUDE. Of course there are those who have assisted us in
numerous ways towards the finality of this work; to them, as ONE, we also beg
their further understanding in not being able to list each person separately
as he or she is so richly deserving."Last," but in no sense of this word's
classical meaning, we wish to thank those many friends who have constantly
criticized our work here at Alkebu-lan Books Associates in order that we
maintain our high standards of serving African (BLACK) peoples everywhere in
this "CULTURAL REVOLUTION" - The First Step To Mental Freedom and Physical
Nationhood.

Yosef ben-Jochannan
and
George E. Simmonds
September, 1971

HAM The son of Noah, cursed for spying on his drunken father's nakedness (GENESIS 9:20-25). He was the father of Cush, Mizrain, Punt, and Canaan.

> (from Donald T. Kauffman, THE DICTIONARY
> OF RELIGIOUS TERMS, Westwood, New Jersey,
> 1967, p. 222)

HAMITE Native of North Africa believed to have descended from Noah's son Ham.

> (ibid., p. 225)

Note: "Cush" (Ethiopia), "Punt" (Puanit or Kenya and Somaliland), and "Canaan" (the land the Hebrews, or Jews, stole from its former owners after exterminating them) are not in North Africa. These two conflicting RACIST and RELIGIOUSLY BIGOTED entries best exemplify the purpose for this work. Compare these two quotations with those on pages xii, 29 (bottom quotation) and 30.

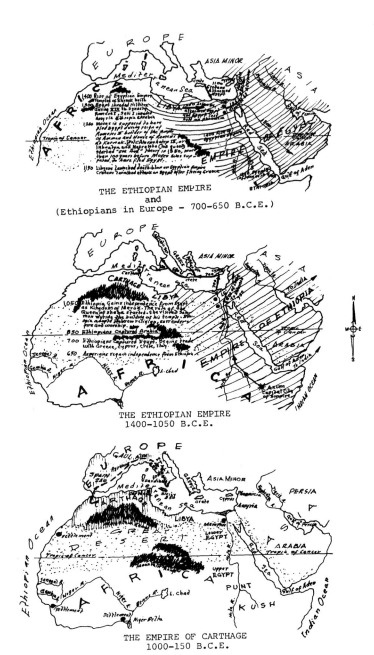

THE ETHIOPIAN EMPIRE
and
(Ethiopians in Europe - 700-650 B.C.E.)

THE ETHIOPIAN EMPIRE
1400-1050 B.C.E.

THE EMPIRE OF CARTHAGE
1000-150 B.C.E.

xx

CAUCASIAN, SEMITIC, HAMITIC, NORTH and EAST AFRICA?
(The World's Most Modern Racist Myth)

## SEMITICISM'S CHAMPIONS

On page 485 of the late professor James Henry Breasted's book, THE CON-
QUEST OF CIVILIZATION (a new and fully revised edition by Edith Williams Ware,
Ph.D.), the following appears:

> ...There were now but two rivals in the Western Mediterranean
> world - Rome and Carthage. In the following inevitable strug-
> gle of these two for the mastery of the Western Mediterranean
> during the next two generations, we shall be watching the final
> conflict between the western wings of the two far-reaching
> racial lines, the Semitic and the Indo-European.

As we open our SAFARI (excursion) into the heritage of one of Africa's
indigenous peoples, in this case the Khart Haddans, otherwise called "CARTHA-
GINIANS" by European-American "educators," the entire basis for "Western
"WHITE RACISM and RELIGIOUS BIGOTRY" unleach their ugly venomous poison from
the pen of one of the United States of America's "...GREATEST ANTHROPOLOGISTS
OF ALL TIMES," James Henry Breasted, and/or one of his many well-disciplined
students - Edith Williams Ware. But; why did the author find it necessary to
make these indigenous Ethiopians (Africans of Khart Haddas) "SEMITIC"? Because
his, or her, so-called "...INDO-EUROPEAN...RACIAL LINES..." called out to remember that the Romans (a branch of the "Indo-Europeans") were at one time the
SLAVES of the Africans ("NEGROES") of Carthage - during the Second Khart Haddan
Wars (Carthage vs. Rome), the so-called "PUNIC WARS," about c. 220 B.C.E.

One could assume by the above revelations that professor Breasted made the
Carthaginians relatives of the "SEMITIC" PEOPLE, but not of the "INDO-
EUROPEANS" (the Caucasians). Obviously the good professor did not feel that
European and European-American (White) Jews are, or were, CAUCASIANS like
himself; as he declared that "SEMITIC" peoples are of different "...RACIAL
LINES..." than "CAUCASIANS." Here we can clearly observe how RACISM and
RELIGIOUS BIGOTRY take strange turns against their progenitors!

Upon what historical evidence did professor Breasted draw his RACIAL conclusion that the Ethiopians ("Negroes, Bantus," etc.) of Carthage were
"SEMITIC"? What is he inferring; that the pitiful group of followers who
migrated from Phoenicia with their Princess Elissar (Virgil's DIDO), at

1

approximately c. 1000 or c. 900 B.C.E.,[4] amalgamation with the so-called
"NEGROES" of Khart Haddas caused the "NEGROES" to become "PHOENICIANS" -
otherwise "SEMITIC"? If this be TRUE, it is obvious that the professor, and/or
Dr. Ware, must have been in contact with some kind of secret information
available to themselves and not to the ancient Europeans of the Mediterranean,
particularly the Greeks and Romans who wrote about the ancient Ethiopians or
Africans ("NEGROES") of North Africa without mention of any "SEMITIC PEOPLES"
of Carthage, or of any other part of North or East Africa.

On page 505 of the same book,[5] professor Breasted and/or Dr. Ware displayed another aspect of their apparent RACISM when they wrote the following
about the <u>African General of Carthage</u> - Hannibal Barca:

> Thus this masterful young Carthaginian, the greatest of
> Semite generals, within two years after his arrival in Italy
> and before he was thrity years of age, had defeated his
> giant antagonist in four battles and destroyed three of the
> opposing armies.

If there is any doubt as to why Breasted or Ware had to make the Carthaginians "SEMITIC," it should be dispelled by the last quotation above. But
one must question whether the professor or his attendant was aware of the
existence of the following coins showing the likeness of General Hannibal
Barca's face from a side view on one side of the coin, and an elephant on the
opposite side. Coins of this vintage were freely used during the period when
General Barca was at his zenith as conqueror of the Iberian Peninsula (Spain,
Portugal and part of southern France), the regions of the Alps Mountain ranges
and the Po River Valley, also all of northern Italy. In all of these conquests
his African ("NEGRO") troops (soldiers), not WARRIORS, over sixty thousand
(60,000) of them, <u>mated freely</u> with Breasted's and Ware's "...INDO-EUROPEAN"
female captives; the same as European-Americans of the British colonies that
became the United States of America <u>mated freely</u> with their "NEGRO SLAVES"

(*See C. T. Seltman, GREEK COINS: A History of Metalic Currency and Coinage
down to the fall of the Hellenistic Kingdoms, London, 1933; also J. A. Rogers,
SEX AND RACE, New York, 1967, Vol. I.)

from all over the continent of Africa - many of them descendants of Carthaginians. It must be noted that Europeans and European-Americans also "RAPED"
their "NEGRO SLAVES" and "COLONIALS" in Africa from the beginning of the
ATLANTIC SLAVE TRADE in 1503 C.E. to the present day. The coins on the preceding page are only two of the many types minted by the Khart Haddans for
General Barca.

For other pictures of the above coins see page 81 of Joel A. Rogers,
SEX AND RACE, New York, 1954, vol. I; Frank M. Snowden's, BLACKS IN ANTIQUITY:
A CRECO-ROMAN EXPERIENCE, Harvard University Press, Cambridge, 1970; and Yosef
ben-Jochannan's, BLACK MAN OF THE NILE, Alkebu-lan Books Associates, New York,
1970, p. 198 (bottom numbers). But, what is there about the above coins that
is "SEMITIC" in character with respect to General Hannibal Barca's face that
is not, also, called "NEGRO," or even "NEGROID"? Certainly the facial characteristics are similar to those Herodotus and all of the other ancient Greeks,
as well as the Romans, called "ETHIOPIAN FEATURES." There is no appearance of
the so-called "TYPICAL SEMITIC NOSE" one hears so much about of late; instead,
it is typical of the so-called "NEGRO'S BROAD NOSE" and "WOOLLY HAIR" one
sees in the Harlems of the United States of America each and every day of each
and every year. Thus; can it be said that the good professor's statement is
basically different than the position taken by another so-called "AFRICANIST"
- Basil Davidson, in his book, THE AFRICAN PAST, page 46, in which he differed
with Herodotus' first-hand physical description of the indigenous Africans
of Egypt and other lands of North and East Africa, and of lands even around
Greece - Colchis? Herodotus wrote about them in the following manner:

> THE ETHIOPIANS, COLCHIANS AND EGYPTIANS HAVE THICK LIPS,
> BROAD NOSE, WOOLLY HAIR, AND THEY ARE BURNT OF SKIN.

Basil Davidson, on the other hand, objected to any "RACIAL" significance in
Herodotus' description; and cited that:

> ...On circumcision, for example, "as between the Egyptians
> and the Ethiopians that is, the Kushites, I should not like
> to say which learned from the other..." As to the skin color
> of the Egyptians, he recalls the story of a dove connected
> with the Egyptian oracle at Dodona. This bird was said to
> have been black. Why black? "As to the bird being black,"
> says Herodotus, "they merely signify by this that the woman
> was an Egyptian." Explaining why the Colchians "are of

Egyptian descent," he suggests that they may have descended from Egyptian soldiers who had served under
Sesostris, a Pharaoh whose armies had invaded the Near
East. But "my own idea on the subject was based first on
the fact that they the Colchians have black skins and
woolly ahir (not that it amounts to much, as other nations
have the same), and secondly, and more especially, on the
fact that the Colchians, the Egyptians, and the Ethiopians
the Kushites are the only races which from ancient times
have practiced circumcision." "Black" notwithstanding, it
will be rash to build any "racial" conclusions from this
much-commented passage: what interested Herodotus was not
"racial" origins of the people but their habits and relationships.

I have carefully underlined what the so-called "WHITE LIBERAL AFRICANISTS"

would prefer that BLACK PEOPLE forget about Herodotus' description of the

Africans and Europeans during his era. Herodotus was most certainly interested

in "RACE" and "HABITS" of the people he was speaking about; also in their

"COLOR," which he used in identifying the Africans. What Herodotus wrote around

c. 457 or 450 B.C.E. remains to haunt and taunt the professional "SEMITISTS"

and so-called "AUTHORITIES ON AFRICAN HISTORY AND CULTURE," Basil Davidson

"NOTWITHSTANDING." His conclusion was no better than that of another so-called

"AUTHORITY ON AFRICA" - C. G. Seligman - whom he criticized on page 37 of the

same book.[6] Davidson wrote:

> The same distinctive attitude of the nineteenth century
> may be seen at a more sophisticated level in the approach
> of early anthropologists, believing as they generally did
> that Africa was some kind of "human reserve" where the
> nature and condition of Ancient Man could be studied in
> all its simplicity and savage innocence: a reserve, more-
> over, in which the Negroes occupied the lowest place in the
> hierarchy of achievement, while the "Hamites" (honorary
> Europeans, being of caucasoid origin) were responsible, in
> the words of no less an authority than the late C. G.
> Seligman, for any good thing that might have got itself
> done. "It would be very wide of the mark," wrote Seligman
> some forty years ago, "to say that the history of Africa
> south of the Sahara is no more than the story of the
> permeation through the ages, in different degrees and at
> various times, of the Negro and Bushman aboriginals by
> Hamitic blood and culture." Racialist declarations such
> as this will now seem far from the truth - so far indeed
> that the very existence of ancient "Hamites" in Africa
> south of the Sahara has become a matter of grave scholarly
> doubt - but they were the natural outcome of the Europo-
> centriccentricism which accompanied the years of discovery
> and conquest.

Before I deal with either Davidson or Seligman on the matter of the

indigenous Africans of North and East Africa being either "SEMITES" or "HAMITES;"

I should examine Davidson's own words in his condemnation of his fellow

4

European whom he could not call a RACIST, it would seem, as he was. Instead, he elected to refer to Seligman's RACIST OBSESSION as "EUROPOCENTRICISM." He also writes of European "DISCOVERY." The Europeans did not "DISCOVER" one piece of land nor one human being in the entire world except of Europe and Europeans. Just imagine the Europeans DISCOVERING THE SOURCE OF THE NILE while thousands of Africans who have lived there for generations after generations WATCH THEMSELVES BEING DISCOVERED!

It must be noted that the "SEMITIC" syndrome is not confined to North and East Africa alone. European and European-American "EDUCATORS" geared to racism in history have gone so far with this idiosyncracy that they even claim:

> The people of the west African empires: Ghana, Mali, Songhay, were Negroes but their rulers were white Semites.

The above claim is best stated in E. W. Bovill's, THE GOLDEN TRADE OF THE MOORS (a revised version by Robin Hallett), originally Bovill's GOLDEN TRADE OF OLD SAHARA.[7] On page 69 of the book, they attempted to make us believe that one West African Empire's:

> ...ruling dynasty was white, but the people were black Mandingo.

Bovill was referring to the Ghana Kingdom and Empire that existed long before the turn of the Christian Era (C.E.),[8] which was destroyed around c. 1298 C.E. However Bovill, like most of the other European and European-American "AFRICANISTS" who perpetuate the "SEMITIC NORTH AFRICA" and "HAMITIC EAST AFRICA" myths, did not attempt to present one bit of evidence to support his WHITE and SEMITIC RACISM, especially how "...THE RULING DYNASTY..." of Ghana, Mali and Songhay became "WHITE;" or when the "...WHITE RULERS..." became members of the "...BLACK MANDINGOES..." But why did this type of RACISM go unchallenged for so many generations? Because Bovill, as all of the other "SEMITISTS, HAMITISTS, and CAUCASIANISTS, works only prattle what the vast majority of so-called "WHITE LIBERAL EDUCATORS" have been teaching in each and every institution of "HIGHER LEARNING" throughout Europe, Great Britain, and the United States of America; equally in all of the colonies connected to these imperialist powers.

The following OVERVIEW of the ancient Africans (Ethiopians, "Negroes, Bantus, Africans South of the Sahara, Hottentots, Bushmen, Pygmies," and

5

whatever else Europeans and White Americans call African peoples) of North and
East Africa resulted from a basic need to expose the perpetrators of the
"CAUCASIA-SEMITIC-HAMITIC" syndrome with respect to the Africans who taught
the Greeks and Romans of the ancient Mediterranean "world" how to develop their
own High-Cultures. African teachers of the Greeks and Romans who were called
"ETHIOPIANS OF EGYPT, ETHIOPIANS OF COLCHIS, ETHIOPIANS OF MEROWE, ETHIOPIANS
OF NUBIA, ETHIOPIANS OF CARTHAGE, ETHIOPIANS OF LEBUS, ETHIOPIANS OF WEST
AFRICA, ETHIOPIANS OF EAST AFRICA," and all other sorts of "ETHIOPIANS;" but
never a "NEGRO" - this term being TOTALLY UNKNOWN TO THE ANCIENTS OF AFRICA,
ASIA AND EUROPE.

EXAMINING THE RECORDS

Let us examine the records of mankind's antiquitous history in a manner
whereby those of us who comprise what has been generally characterized as
"...THE LITERATE BUT UNEDUCATED MASSES..." can understand. We shall not look
at the facts as "CLASSICAL HISTORIANS, ACADEMICIANS, AUTHORITIES," or even
"SCHOLARS," but as "TRUTH SEEKERS." Where shall we begin this educational
SAFARI with respect to the first so-called "SEMITIC PEOPLES" in order to find
the earliest reference to them historically before 19th and 20th century
"EDUCATORS" of the "Semitic" and "Caucasian" WESTERN WORLD (Western Civilization) even created the term "RACE"? The first records of people under this
RACIAL classification, "SEMITES" we find in the writings of Europeans and
European-Americans of the middle-19th century C.E. (A.D.). These writers have
been given the name "SEMITISTS" by their academic colleagues; but I prefer to
call them "SEMITICISTS" in order that the full impact of the entire first part
of this RACIST and RELIGIOUSLY BIGOTED term can be observed at all times. Thus
we have the following historical background: "SEMITIC," from the mythical "son
of Noah, SEM" or SHEM. From "SEM" came his, and his father Noah (or Noe),
equally mythical descendants - "SEMITES." And lastly; those closely related to
this mythical "RACIAL LINE" became "SEMITIC PEOPLES." "The first of the
SEMITES," according to the Semiticist educators of every discipline connected
to Africa's High-Cultures, arrived in Kimit (Sais or Egypt) as conquerors
around the period beginning with the 17th Dynasty - c. 1675 B.C.E. During this

6

During this period the indigenous Africans of Egypt, many of whom are shown in the following pages, were still referring to their indigenous homeland as KIMIT, and to themselves as ROMITI (Romitu, singular). These allegedly "SEMITIC PEOPLES" most "Western historians" claimed came from an area around the banks of the OXUS RIVER in Asia, somewhere close to the Gulf of Persia (today's Iran). Then, following these were the "PERSIANS THAT INVADED AND CONQUERED EGYPT IN c. 525 B.C." And, that a handful of "nomadic people" from ASIA, called at the time "HARIBU" (today misnomered "Jews"), also entered shortly after the Hyksos invaders with their "LEADER" (a shepherd herder), a man they called "AVRAM" (Abram or Abraham), at approximately c. 1630 B.C.E. (B.C.). For proof of this they cited the "FIRST BOOK OF MOSES," also known as the "BOOK OF GENESIS," of the Hebrew or Jewish HOLY TORAH (the Christian's "OLD TESTAMENT"). However, between the period of the first foreign invasion against a nation on the continent of Africa by so-called "SEMITES" - the Hyksos - to the period of the ARAB-MUSLIM invaders from the Arabian Peninsula of southwestern Asia in 640 C.E. (A.D. or 18 A.H.), there were other encroachments on Egyptian (African) soil by other Asians from Assyria in c. 633 B.C.E., Persians in c. 525 B.C.E.; also from Europe    - Greeks in c. 332 B.C.E., and Romans in c. 47 B.C.E. All of these foreign invasions added to the amalgamation of the indigenous Africans who originally settled Kimit, all of which caused a basic change in the general physical characteristics and color ("RACE," according to anthropologists and paleontologists) of the Egyptian Africans. But the effects of said amalgamation was not sufficient to the point where Herodotus and other ancient Greeks and Romans  could not describe them, even hundreds of years later, as "ETHIOPIANS, BLACKS," etc. (the term "NEGRO" being not yet invented). Needless to say that between the foreign invasions from Asia and Europe, there were others from African nations within the continent of Africa. However, Africans from THEBES tried to assist their Egyptian brethren in driving out the Assyrians that defeated them when they were ruling Egypt. Africans from NUBIA and ITIOPI (Kush or Ethiopia) also tried to drive out the Persians when they were ruling Egypt. But, the latter two invasions by the indigenous Africans in defense of their Egyptian brothers and sisters met with

7

QUEEN TIYI, mother of Akhenaton
(Berlin Museum)

An Egyptian Princess of the 18th Dynasty
(Berlin Museum)

AMENOPHIS III, father of Akhenaton, and
mighty conqueror (Berlin Museum)

A daughter of Akhenaton, and a sister of
Tut-Ankh-Amen (Cairo Museum)

a

b

devastating defeats at the hands of the so-called "SEMITIC" invaders - the
Assyrians and Persians (foreigners from Asia). During the course of these
contacts between Africans, Asians, and Europeans, the ancient Romans and
Greeks continued calling the indigenous Africans of Egypt and other areas of
Africa they met - "ETHIOPIANS" or "BLACKS," according to all of the Greek and
Roman works of that period in world history dealing with the continent of
Africa and all of its indigenous people. The name, "ETHIOPIAN," was given to
all of Africa's people before Homer wrote his ILLIAD and ODYSSEY around c. 600
B.C.E.; at least it was being used during Homer's lifetime, as he used that
term several times in the two works mentioned. The "Ethiopians" mentioned
by him, as by thousands of other ancients before, during, and after, him were
similar to the "ETHIOPIANS, BLACKS," or even "NEGROES", shown on the following
page of this work; all of them taken from the pages of volumes of works by
European "scholars" with nothing to be afraid of in saying that they were
"NEGROES" by the millions in the indigenous history of the "MEDITERRANEAN
WORLD" - particularly in Greece and Rome.

We have observed that the first non-Egyptian Africans (politically only)
that captured Egypt after the original settlers arrived from parts around
the African Great Lakes region were the Lebians from Lebus (Libyans from Libya),
North Africa, west of Egypt,[10] in approximately c. 950 B.C.E. Also, that these
people Herodotus, and other ancient Mediterraneans, described as bearing the
same physical resemblance to their Egyptian brothers and sisters. The second
group was the KUSHITES and NUBIANS (jointly) in approximately c. 751 B.C.E.;
they also have been described by Herodotus and other ancients in the same
manner they described the Egyptians and Lebians - as "ETHIOPIANS" or "BLACKS."
Why? Because there were no major physical differences mentioned by the ancient
Romans and Greeks between the NUBIANS, EGYPTIANS, KUSHITES, LEBIANS, KHART
HADDANS (Carthaginians), PUANITS (Punts), NUMIDIANS or GARAMANTES, as there
is today on the part of so-called modern "EGYPTOLOGISTS, AUTHORITIES ON AFRICA,
SEMITICISTS, HAMITICISTS, WHITE LIBERAL HISTORIANS, AFFICANISTS," and the likes
of them. Yet, the "NUBIANS" were, supposedly, the only indigenous Ethiopians
(Blacks) the "NEGROPHOBES" conceded were "N=E=G=R=O=E=S"* - whatever this

disgusting and nauseating term meant to the 16ᵗʰ or 17ᵗʰ century Portuguese
RACISTS that invented it; a term which some of the world's greatest "SEMITI-
CISTS" and "CAUCASIANISTS" even breakdown to make the NUBIANS appear as
"HAMITIC-TYPE CAUCASIANS, DARK-SKINNED CAUCASOIDS" and "NILOTIC HAMITES."

Was it Herodotus alone, of the ancients, that described the Ethiopians,
or "Negroes," of North Africa and the Nile Valley (Blue and White) High-
Cultures in the manner outlined so far? No; not by the slightest stretch of
one's imagination. Xenophanes, Democritus, Strabo, Diodorus and Diogenes
Laertius, all of them ancient Greeks of noted "scholarship" to whom most
Europeans and European-Americans owe their knowledge of the arts and sciences
which came to them by way of the Africans of the Nile Valley, Great Lakes
regions, North Africa, and other parts of the African (Ethiopian or Alkebu-lan)
continent, held to the exact description of the Africans of their era (and
Herodotus') and did not exclude any group of Africans from said COLOR and
PHYSICAL (RACIAL) identification.

We are now confronted with the new approach by the so-called "LIBERAL
WHITE AFRICANISTS" of the late 20ᵗʰ century C.E., such as Basil Davidson's
vintage. In the latter's case, we find him opposing Herodotus' physical description of the Egyptians, Colchians, and Ethiopians as non-RACIAL in the
modern usage of the term "RACE." But Herodotus was describing the Africans
he met and lived amongst, besides being taught by them around c. 457-50 B.C.E.,
not one of whom Basil Davidson or any other of the modern "WHITE LIBERAL
HISTORIANS" or "AFRICANISTS" ever met. Davidson even tried to edit-out the
TRUE meaning of the ancients', particularly Herodotus', "RACIAL" (physical)
descriptions of the Africans of North, East and Central-East Africa.

Before dealing directly with Davidson, and others like him, let us first
examine some of the facts related to Herodotus' (and others) description of
the Africans of North, East, West, South and Central Africa, those of Colchis
in Eur-Asia, and of Persia and India, which included those of the ancient home
of the "modern SEMITICISTS" - Palestine (part of today's State of Israel).

---

*See Richard B. Moore, THE WORD NEGRO, ITS ORIGIN AND EVIL USE, New York, c1954,
for a detailed historical analysis of this word; also the following map from
Y. ben-Jochannan, BLACK MAN OF THE NILE, New York, 1970, pp. 266-67 bottom.

"The Vision of Isaiah." The Hebrew Prophet portrayed as an African BLACK MAN. (reproduced from a 5th century A.D. Greek manuscript). — Biblio-Nationale, Paris, France.

11

Even Greece, Rome, and other lands on the European side of the Mediterranean seaboard (all the way to the PILLARS OF HERCULESE - the Rock of Gibraltar, Gibral Tarikh or Tarikh Rock) are included in this examination or Safari (Excursion). For unlike Davidson, and others such as professor James H. Breasted, C. G. Seligman, and Donald C. Weidner, the ancients also wrote about the "Ethiopians" who even "sailed through the PILLARS OF HERCULESE" to establish contact with their fellow-Ethiopians on the West Coast of Africa; all of which dispell the BIG LIE we have been taught about "the Africans fear of entering the Atlantic Ocean" (formerly Ethiopian Ocean) for fear of "falling over its table-top surface." In this regard Palaephatus tells us that the same type of "Ethiopians" ("Negroes") invaded and captured CERENE, an island off the coast of the PILLARS OF HERCULESE - today's Rock of Gibraltar.[11] Palaephatus was one of the most noted Greek historians of the 4th century B.C.E. ("before the Christian era, or B.C.").[12] In this area of Greek reporting, the records left by an African admiral, Hanno of Khart Haddas (Carthage), commissioned by Pharaoh Necho (Herodotus' "Necos"), about his voyage to CERENE around the 6th or 7th century B.C.E., do justice to the Greeks' (such as Palaephatus) writings that were considered "OFFICIAL" up until the 4th century B.C.E. - at least. The extent of Admiral Hanno's influence on the ancient Greeks and Romans was such that in their historical analysis of a 4th century B.C.E. work, THE PERIPLUS OF SCYLAX,[13] they described CERENE in exactly the same words used by the admiral:

> Cerene is the major trading place, where Ethiopian-Carthaginians and Ethiopians of West Africa met to barter their leopards, lions, precious stones, jewelry, wine, perfume, and Athenian pottery.[14]

It must be emphasized that Scylax was very much aware of the "Ethiopians," the so-called "Negroes," of his era, as he was one of the first to go beyond Herodotus' physical ("RACIAL") description of the Ethiopians; with respect to facial characteristics only. He even described the Ethiopians of West Africa as "...THE TALLEST AND MOST GOOD-LOOKING OF MEN." Yet, to some extent Scylax relied very heavily on Herodotus' description.[1] Xenophanes, on the other hand, was much more specific than both of them, stating that what mis-educators of the 20th century call "SEMITES" or "EGYPTIANS" were:

12

...BLACK-FACED WITH FLAT NOSE...

Some of the "modern historians" claimed that <u>Xenophanes was the first to use</u> <u>physical characteristics as a point of racial identification of the Ethiopians</u> rather than color of skin.[15] Of this point, I cannot subscribe; for, what was it but "PHYSICAL CHARACTERISTICS when Herodotus wrote that:

> ...the Colchians, Ethiopians and Egyptians have the most woolly-hair of all mankind...?

It should be noted also that Herodotus classified the indigenous Ethiopians of Libya in the same manner. And, there could be no doubt that Herodotus (in c. 457-450 B.C.E.) knew both the Libyans and Egyptians[16] as much as he did the Kushites and Nubians. About the Kushites, he even described their "...<u>land</u> <u>to the south of Egypt</u>..." from whence they came. He placed its geo-political boundary as follows:

> (a) Merowe or Meroe, its capital,[17] at two travel - distance - from the city of Elephantine.
> (b) At two months travel along the White Nile at a southwesterly direction from Merowe.

Herodotus also divided the Ethiopians into "MACROBIANS, ASMACHIANS" and "CAVE DWELLERS." As far as he was concerned, obviously, all of the Ethiopians (Egyptians, Nubians, Carthaginians, Garamantes, Ghanians, Kushites, etc.), at least those he was aware of, were basically the same in physical characteristics ("thick lips, broad nose, woolly hair") and color (black or "burnt skin"). At no instance in his writings did he relate to any of them being SEMITIC or HAMITIC, nor even CAUCASIAN. He was equally certain that many of the Ethiopians could be found in goodly numbers in parts all over the Eastern countries (Arabia Felix - the Arabian Peninsula, Persia, India, etc.).

Herodotus' anthropological description of the Ethiopians (so-called "NEGROES") was not only verified by Aeschylus, who also delineated Ethiopia's geo-political boundaries; he also wrote about the Ethiopians of Kush beliefs and mythology. His details were further supported by the reports of other Greeks and Romans who also dealt with captured Ethiopians following the defeat of Xerxes. But, just like Xenophanes referred to the Ethiopians because of stories he heard about them from his fellow Colophonians, and his own experiences with them, Herodotus also spoke of the:

...BLACK FLATTEN-NOSED ETHIOPIANS I MET...,[18]
etc. Even Strabo 17.1.2 and 17.1.5 cites Eratosthenes' works with regards to
the Egyptians who fought against Cambyses and his Persian invaders of Merowe
being BLACK (Ethiopian); this he wrote about c. 525 B.C.E. Further verifica-
tion came from other Greeks who fought the Ethiopians at the battle of Xerxes.

It is written that "Aeschylus was the first of the Greeks to place the
Ethiopian"Kushites at a specific"geo-political"boundary in Africa." This may
have been very much true; but Ionian merchants and mercenaries who  served in
the army of Psammetiches I (otherwise known as "Psamtik" biblically), somewhere between the years c. 663-609 B.C.E., also described the Ethiopians they
met in Africa, Egypt in particular,[19] with respect to their geo-political
setting.

There could be no doubt that the early Greeks and Romans of Herodotus'
lifetime, and subsequent, or even during the period when Homer wrote his
ILLIAD and ODYSSEY, description of all the Africans they encountered was in
terms of their "BLACK" color of skin. They made many references to the Africans
pigmentation, and of course made distinction in their remarks to the degree of
BLACKNESS or variance of DARKNESS between different national groupings of
Ethiopians ("Negroes" or "BLACKS") on the continent of Africa (Alkebu-lan).
This factor was best observed by Philostratus in his description of "MEMNON"
not being as "...BLACK AS OTHER ETHIOPIANS;" indicating that the Greeks were
quite observant of the variance in degree of BLACKNESS[20] among the Ethiopians.
Roman "scholars," at least quite a few of them, including Statius, suggested
that they were even in contact with a kind of "BLACKISH-RED ETHIOPIANS."[21]
One can still find Africans of "REDDISH," otherwise called "COPPER COLOR" or
"COPPERTONE," hue all over the continent of Africa to this present day.
Hundreds of thousands of said Africans can be found around the Kalahari Desert
of Monomotapa.*

At no time during the earliest period of Greek enlightenment, from Homer
to Herodotus (c. 600-450 B.C.E.) and beyond, has it been shown that the ancient
Greeks referred to the Northern Africans in question as anything other than

---

*Ancient name for the southernmost part of Africa, today wrongfully called
"THE REPUBLIC OF SOUTH AFRICA."

"ETHIOPIANS," so far as COLOR and RACIAL CHARACTERISTICS are concerned. The words "SEMITIC" and "SEMITES," nor anything close to them, were not yet invented. This was true even to the days of the Ptolemies - General Soter or Ptolemey I (c. 327) to Ptolmey XV (c. 47 B.C.E.). One of them wrote that the Ethiopians of the lands around and about Merowe were of the "BLACKEST" and "PUREST" type. Thus we also find Philo indicating that "...MOSES'" (the indigenous Ethiopian of Egypt who gave his fellow religious cohorts works from the BOOK OF THE DEAD and the NEGATIVE CONFESSIONS - from whence the TEN COMMANDMENTS were taken) "WIFE," a Kushite or Ethiopian, "WAS EXCEEDINGLY BLACK." Philo's conclusion certainly raised quite a lot of RACIAL problems for our "modern SEMITICISTS" who would prefer that the so-called "PEOPLE OF THE BOOK" remain "WHITE SEMITES."

What we have seen so far is that the ancient peoples of the Europeans side of the Mediterranean Sea, particularly the Greeks and Romans - the first of the Europeans to be CULTURED by Asians and Africans, did not speak or write of the "NEGROES" (which they called "Ethiopians" and/or "Africans") of their era in terms of racial expressions such as "CAUCASIAN, CAUCASOID, SEMITIC, HAMITIC" and "NEGROID," but as "BLACK" at the extreme North, "BLACKER" and "BLACKEST" below the areas of the North that were closest to the equator; the ancient Europeans not knowing the difference between geographic boundaries of Africa (Ethiopia) that far South at that time in history. (See the following maps on page 16 extracted from page 118 - top or 134 bottom of BLACK MAN OF THE NILE, New York, 1970. Take careful notation of the remarks below the maps). Even the so-called "SEMITIC NOSE" one hears so much about of late, which was rejected for centuries by the ancestors of most who now consider it of greatest importance to prove their "SEMITIC HERITAGE," was not mentioned by any of the ancients; this, too, being a development of the modern RACISTS and RELIGIOUS BIGOTS from the inception of their projection of anthropology and paleontology as the panacea that proves the superiority of the "INDO-EUROPEAN RACES," Semites included, over all other "RACES;" the latter conclusion perpetuated to the limit in European-America, and to a very great extent in European-controlled areas of South and Central America - which also includes the islands of the Caribbean Sea.

15

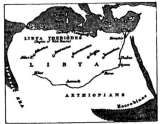

AFRICA ACCORDING TO ERATOSTHENES 200 B.C.E.

AFRICA ACCORDING TO HERODOTUS 450 B.C.E.

Note that Eratosthenes and Herodotus, as well as other
Europeans of their era, believed that the Sahara was
"a great body of water" (ocean or lake). They had no
conception of "Africa South of the Sahara." To date this
general conception, though somewhat changed, still
carries the same old stereotype connotations. Yet, they
had turned the "HORN" (at ancient Punt, present-day
Somali) of East Africa and entered the Indian Ocean.
However; they had no conception of West, Central,
South or Southeast Africa, as indicated by these two
maps. And these are the best and most accurate of
that era.

The MYTH of a "SEMITIC" or "CAUCASIAN" indigenous North Africa is no less

RACIST in its intent than the current projection of a "WHITE (native) AFRICA"

and "BLACK AFRICA" South of the Sahara. For example: in Elsy Leuzinger's book,

THE ART OF AFRICA,[22] under the heading on page 223 ..."Tables of African Races

And Cultures"..., the following appears:

(Based on H. Bavmann, Volkerkunde von Africa, greatly
simplified)

I. WHITE AFRICA

Mediterranean, Ethiopia, Semitic and Cro-Magnon races.
Advanced cultures, oriented towards the Mediterranean
and the Orient, in the sub-tropical region.
Egypt, the Sahara and area of the Atlas mountains:
river valley, desert and highlands with mountain ranges

and salt steppe. Oasis agriculture with artificial
irrigation, ploughing and hoeing; pastoral cultures.

### II. BLACK AFRICA
### A - Negroes

1. SUDANESE CULTURES (from the borders of the
Guinea lands to the Upper Nile, and from the
Sahara and Sahel to the Congo forests): Sudanese
and Nilotic races, with an Ethiopian admixture.
Old Nigritic patriarchial culture, with a Hamitic
upper class.

The above RACIST categorization of Africa's indigenous people continues
on page 225 in the following manner:

### B - Non-Negro Peoples of Black Africa

1. EASTERN HAMITIC CATTLE-BREEDERS (East Africa,
including Ethiopia, and scattered over the whole
of South and West Africa): Ethiopian upper stratum,
pure or intermixed with negroids: Hamito-Nilotes.
Pastoral culture, with large-size cattle (in part
as overlords over Old Nigritic settlers and remnants
of hunting peoples).

Further quotations of this alleged AUTHORITY ON AFRICA at this point would be
useless, in so far as the RACIST mania is concerned. I do hope, however, that
you can further see why it is necessary to point out that the so-called
"NEGROES," or even the above "OLD NIGRITIC" people, are, and have always been,
indigenous to all of the continent of Alkebu-lan (Ethiopia, Africa, or else.
See map on page 18 for other names "AFRICA" was called by the ancients). Of
course the so-called "PYGMIES OF THE CONGO JUNGLES," allegedly "a distinctly
separate RACE from the NEGRITI and the BANTU, equally the BUSHMEN and the
HOTTENTOT of the salt steppes and semi-deserts of southern Africa," had to be
the originators of the "SEMITES" and "INDO-EUROPEANS" (Caucasians); but why
not of the so-called "AFRICANS SOUTH OF THE SAHARA" - "Black Africa." Maybe
the map on page 18, which was created by another of the perpetrators of the
"CAUCASIAN NORTH AFRICA" syndrome, Dr. Donald Wiedner, demonstrates this point
much better than I can tell. Here you see how this alleged authority on Africa
has removed each and everyone of his so-called "NEGROES" from North Africa
before 300 B.C.E. Obviously someone needs to present this ethnographer with
works on this topic from the ancient Europeans of the Mediterranean. A copy
of a modern scholar's book, Frank Snowden's, BLACKS OF ANTIQUITY: A Greco-
Roman Experience, Harvard University (Belknap Press), Cambridge, 1970,

# Of MAP AFRICA.
### 1 6 8 B.C.E.

A FRICA, by the Ancients, was called *Olympia, Hesperia, Oceania, Coryphe, Ammonia, Ortygia,* and *Æthiopia.* By the *Greeks* and *Romans, Lybia* and *Africa.* By the *Æthiopians* and *Moors, Alkebu-lan.*

Note: European colonialists from the 15ᵗʰ through 19ᵗʰ century, C.E. refused to accept their ignorance of Africa's interior and made all sorts of maps with waterways, mountains, nations and peoples which did not exist on the continent.

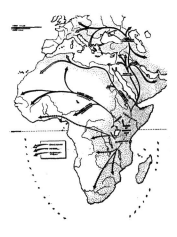

**ETHNOGRAPHY OF AFRICA** BEFORE 300 B.C. *(HYPOTHESIS)*

(Above:) From Donald L. Wiedner, "A History of Africa South of the Sahara," Vintage Book (Alfred A. Knof, Inc., and Random House, Inc.), New York, 1962. (See pp. 7, 9, 23 and compare).

should also help him with his North African _ethnology._

The most ironic aspect of the general "SEMITIC NORTH AFRICA" myth, not to exclude its equally ridiculous partner - "CAUCASIAN NORTH AFRICA," which was 'NEGRO-LESS,' is the fact that all of this "NEGROPHOBIA" rests solely upon a period in North Africa's history of antiquity, when the first of the foreign invaders from Asia - the Hyksos - arrived in northern Kimit (Egypt) as conquerors. Before this period in mankind's history, approximately c. 1675 B.C.E., as I have shown previously, there is no evidence suggestive of any major migration of so-called "SEMITIC PEOPLES" from Asia moving into North or East Africa; even "EGYPTOLOGISTS" and "AFRICANISTS" cannot supply any such information. This is not to say that most of them have not tried, in vain, to do so. Not even their most favorite "INDO-EUROPEANS" have they been able to place in North Africa through migration during that period from their heretofore-claimed indigenous "CAUCASUS MOUNTAINS." How, then, was it possible for the so-called "SEMITIC CAUCASIAN PEOPLES OF EGYPT," and all other parts of North, Northeast, East, and Southeast Africa, were able to co-mingle with the "ETHIOPIANS OF NORTH AFRICA,"[23] Nubians included, and still remain perfectly PURE whatever they were supposed to have been when they arrived? What the SEMITICISTS have not clarified is, how was it possible for Africa to have produced "PURELY DIFFERENT RACES" that were not related to each other biologically, socially, and politically? What natural barriers existed in any of these areas of North and East Africa that suggest North or East of the Zaara (Sahara or Great Desert), Africa's indigenous people lived integratedly, except those whom modern RACISTS and NEGROPHOBES have given the title "AFRICANS SOUTH OF THE SAHARA" or "BANTUS" - sometimes _"Negroes"_ - and even "NIGGERS"? Nothing more than ethnocentrically oriented minds bent upon a dream of a "PURE CAUCASIAN" or a "SEMITIC _race_ could have produced such a conclusion.[24] Do not forget the physical description and color of the indigenous Africans detailed by the ancient Europeans before, and after, Homer to Herodotus - c. 600 to c. 450 B.C.E. Their description refuted this type of distortion of mankind's history; particularly the history and heritage of African people presently marked for CULTURAL GENOCIDE, if not PHYSICAL GENOCIDE, both having been visited upon

African people all over the European and European-American "JUDAEO-CHRISTIAN WORLD" - whatever this is. Of course similar types of RACIAL, CULTURAL and RELIGIOUS discrimination against African people were practiced by Asians (Black and Brown) "MUSLIMS" under the name of Arabians - the latter also masquerading under the banner established by their Indo-European (Caucasian) overlords; thus the term "HAMITIC PEOPLES."

What kind of teaching developed the type of mentality exhibited in the above RACIST and RELIGIOUSLY BIGOTED philosophy of life? We can best see the answer in the "CHOSEN PEOPLE" myth of the Jewish (Haribu or Hebrew) HOLY TORAH (Christian's OLD TESTAMENT); a story connected to the Hebrew God - YHWH (Jehovah). This myth has become part and parcel of every microscopic bits of the fabric of what is better known as the "AMERICAN DREAM;" a "DREAM" in which the victims are still the Africans - "ETHIOPIANS, BLACKS, AFRICANS SOUTH OF THE SAHARA, NEGROES," and even "NIGGERS." It is most commonly prevalent in any of the so-called "Judaeo-Christian Anglo-Saxon Greek Oriented Society," particularly here in these United States of America. All of its ramifications are otherwise called "WESTERN DEMOCRACY" and/or "WESTERN CIVILIZATION;" the assumption being that "Western Civilization" is solely the creation of CAUCASIANS of Indo-European Aryan and Semitic origin.

Since the "SEMITIC" Hyksos did not appear in any capacity of strength in Egypt (North Africa) prior to the 17th Pharonic Dynasty (c. 1675 B.C.E.), and very little or nothing written about them before this period by any of the indigenous Ethiopians (Blacks or "Negroes") of Egypt; why are we still to presume that the Ethiopians of Egypt (Romiti, Romitu singular) were also "SEMITES" before the arrival of the Hyksos from Asia? The answer is very obvious. In most of the United States of America's textbooks written about African people, with hardly any exception, White "educators," many of whom are otherwise called "SCHOLARS," along with their "Negro" subservients, have over-loaded Africa's history with their "SEMITIC NORTH AFRICA" syndrome; much of this due to their need to prove that both JEHOVAH and JESUS CHRIST were, or are, "PURE" CAUCASIANS or SEMITES, each God being "THE ONLY TRUE ONE" (depending upon which part of the ETHNOCENTRICITY a particular "scholar" adhere's to). But before the need for this type of RACIAL identity with a JUDAEO-CHRISTIAN GOD became the obsession it is at present, theologians and historians ("educators" as they call themselves, Christians and Jews alike) wrote that the Hyksos were:

> ................chiefs of the many different Asiatic tribes banded together..............................

The above quotation is taken from Hayes' comments in the CAMBRIDGE ANCIENT HISTORY, vol. II, Cambridge, 1962. Certainly Hayes is one of the "authorities on Africa," an "Africanist" like Basil Davidson, Donald Weidner, James H. Breasted, and all of the men and women of Europe and European-America who have adopted the cloak of protection - "LIBERAL WHITE HISTORIAN."

J. M. Munn-Rankin, another of the so-called "EGYPTOLOGISTS," in his book - IRAQ, 18 (1956), 68ff, inferred that the ..."LATE HYKSOS" vanished into thin air. And, that the "SEMITIC" and "PROVEN EGYPTIAN NAMES" shown in "CARTOUCHES"* during the 17th Dynastic Period, the so-called "HYKSOS PERIOD," have to be further researched from evidence found in the deluge of the confusion that was the feudal Middle Bronze Age. What Munn-Rankin failed to note is, there is no proof (whatsoever) that the Hyksos rule over Egypt ever extended deep into its interior-reaches along the Nile River Valley, beyond what is today called "THE DELTA." And, that most of them did not even know where the first CATARACT was geographically located. Thus, the amalgamation of the Ethiopian peoples of Egypt farther SOUTH of the first CATARACT with the Hyksos is just a matter of a figment of the mind of the perpetuators who peddle the CAUCASIAN and SEMITIC North Africa myth; very sick minds at that. This fact held true, even until the invasion of Egypt by so-called "INDO-EUROPEAN FORCES" under Alexander II ("the great," son of Phillip of Macedonia) in c. 332 B.C.E.; at which time Europeans were able to fully plagiarize the Africans' heritage in Egypt (Kimit, Sais, Mizram or Mizrair) itself.

Why did Manetho, the African High Priest of Greek-controlled Egypt during the reign of Pharaoh Soter I,[24] not refer to the Hyksos foreigners as "SEMITES" or "CAUCASIANS" in his CHRONOLOGY OF THE DYNASTIC PHARAOHS? Even Eusebius, who,

---

* 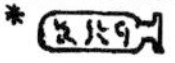 a bottle-like symbol the ancient Nile Valley people used for distinguishing the names and titles of royalty.

like Manetho, published a CHRONOLOGICAL LISTING OF THE PHARONIC DYNASTIES OF
EGYPT, did not indicate in any manner whatsoever that the Hyksos resembled the
indigenous Egyptians (Africans or Ethiopians) in physical characteristics
("THICK LIPS, BROAD NOSE, WOOLLY HAIR"), color ("BURNT SKIN" or "BLACK"), and
religion (worship of the SUPREME GOD Ra). Leo Africanus (Leo the African), also,
like Eusebius and Manetho (with whom he disagreed on their dating of the Hyksos
invasion of Egypt - from the 15th to the 17th dynasties), could not establish a
real "RACIAL" basis similar to the Egyptians for the Hyksos. He felt that:

> ...they were a combination of various Asians much
> more powerful than the Egyptians they conquered,
> but weaker than the Asians they were fleeing.

Gardiner's JOURNAL OF EGYPTIAN ARCHAEOLOGY, 5 (1918), 43, n. 6, cites and
presents Manetho's argument with respect to the CHRONOLOGICAL DATING of the
Hyksos as rulers over Egypt; equally Wadell's, MANETHO, 94. But the much more
modern CHRONOLOGICAL DATING adopted by "western scholars" stems from E. Meyer's
work, Agyptiche Chronologie (Berlin, 1904), 84. Other European works on this
subject one needs to become familiar with are the following: A. Scharff,
Agypten und Vorerasien (Munich, 1950); K. Sethe, Zeitchrift fur Assyriologie
und Verwandite Gebiete (1898), 25ff; Sir Ernest A. Wallis Budge, HISTORY OF
EGYPT (London, 1898); Sir James Frazier, GOLDEN BOUGH (London, 1930), 13 vols.;
and K. C. Seele, WHEN EGYPT RULED THE EAST (Chicago, 1957). The preceding works
are by Europeans, the following by African-Caribbeans and African-Americans:
George G. M. James, STOLEN LEGACY (New York, 1954); John G. Jackson, INTRO-
DUCTION TO AFRICAN CIVILIZATIONS (New York, 1970); Yosef ben-Jochannan, BLACK
MAN OF THE NILE (New York, 1970). I could have mentioned Gaston Maspero's,
HISTORY OF EGYPT (France, 1883); and even A. H. Gardiner's, EGYPT OF THE
PHARAOHS (Oxford, 1961); but, the latter two works seem to be those many of the
present-run of SEMITICISTS quote most frequently. Even Budge, Davidson, Weidner,
Churchward and Frazier quoted Maspero's works as "AUTHORITATIVE."

As I have stated before in many of my other works that preceded this very
short dialogue, the most basic reason for removing the so-called "NEGROES"
from North Africa and East Africa, historically, especially as masters of these
two areas of antiquity, is the fact that said indigenous Ethiopians (Blacks,

etc.) will prove to be the GOD or GODS of indigenous Europeans (Whites, etc.)
- otherwise called "CAUCASIANS, ARYANS, INDO-EUROPEANS, SEMITES," and even
"DARK-SKINNED HAMITIC EUROPEANS" according to C. G. Seligman in his masterpiece
of RELIGIOUS BIGOTRY and SEMITIC RACISM, which he so perfectly demonstrated in
his book, RACES OF AFRICA, New York, 1930 (re-edited and republished in 1969,
each edition holding fast to the "HAMITIC" and "SEMITIC" syndrome). It is
needless to remind you that Seligman's book is still being used as one of the
most "AUTHORITATIVE WORK ON THE RACES OF AFRICA" by many of the so-called
"LIBERAL HISTORIANS" and "BLACK STUDIES PROFESSORS" of European-America today;
all of which appears in their own hypothesis dealing with the notorious prep-
osition of a "WHITE AFRICA" in "BLACK AFRICA," forgetting that the majority
of Europeans and European-Americans, Britishers included, who  comprise the
COLONIES (the so-called "REPUBLIC OF SOUTH AFRICA" also) would have to leave
Africa were it not for the practiced partnership between WHITE-CHRISTIANITY
and WHITE-CAPITALISM backed by GENOCIDE through N.A.T.O.'s military power -
as supported and controlled by the United States of America. But, in spite of
all of this information certain African-American ("Negro") "EDUCATORS" equally
continue their own MIS-EDUCATION of their BLACK brothers and sisters in so-
called "BLACK STUDIES COURSES" taken from books written by SEMITICISTS and
NEGROPHOBES. As such, one can easily find BLACK STUDIES PROFESSORS still
examining how many Nubians were in Egypt of antiquity; and how many of those
who were there came in as slaves. Of course these "NEGRO PROFESSORS" have
never thought of finding out how many CAUCASIANS or SEMITIC PEOPLES were under
the heals of "...THICK LIPS, WOOLLY HAIR, BROAD NOSE, BURNT BLACK..." ("Negro")
pharaohs of Egypt, Nubia and Kush. Moreover, not one of them has dared to
publish a study showing the extent to which Africans of Ethiopians ("NEGROES")
immigrated to ancient Greece and Rome and changed the physical ("RACIAL")
appearance of these two European groups; this being done even before, and
including, the Etruscans. Pages 8 and 11, along with the following page - 24,
are concrete pictorial examples of the AMALGAMATION that took place when the
so-called "NEGROES" were just plain EUROPEANS of the"Mediterranean  World."
You will also notice that these pictures are not new; they have existed for

23

SETI THE GREAT, conqueror of Cush and Assyria and a famous builder, as Amen, the most powerful of the Egyptian gods. (Louvre)

NETEK-AMEN, Nubian Pharaoh, of about 30 B.C. (Lepsius)

NECTANEBO I., statesman and military leader. Opposer of the Assyrian Invaders. 383 B.C. (Turin Museum)

Attic Philosopher from the 4th century BCE, as determined by E. Poulson (Copenhagen, Denmark) as the Greek "Philosopher"PLATO. It appears to be a bust and copy of Silanion after life. The usual busts of Plato are copies of a grave bust made after Plato was already dead for hundreds of years. Note that the tip of the NOSE* has been changed to appear in conformity with what is generally called "DINARIC FORM."

RA-MER-KA AMEN-TARIT, Nubian Pharaoh of about 100 B.C. (Lepsius)

QUEEN NEFERTITI wife of Akhenaton (Berlin Museum)

Mangbetou Queen (Belgian Congo)

*This type of fakery is common with respect to the NOSE and LIPS of thousands of statues taken from the Nile Valleys High-Cultures - Egypt particularly.

generations upon generations in the archives of various "INSTITUTIONS OF HIGHER (mis) LEARNING" throughout Europe, Great Britain, and European-America. Their recent release is to the credit of the so-called "BLACK MILITANT REV-OLUTION" (culturally or physically) underway throughout the entire world where BLACK PEOPLE find themselves entraped by WHITE RACISM and JUDAEO-CHRISTIAN RELIGIOUS BIGOTRY. Yet, the BRAINWASHING continues from a perspective of a LILLY-WHITE HEAVEN and HOLY FAMILY residents; HELL, on the otherhand, being the JET-BLACK DISMAL BURNING PIT with a BLACK and fantastically ugly DEVIL - a SOUL BROTHER of course. None of these descriptions are acceptable. Even if they are understandable, they can never be acceptable to AFRICAN PEOPLES.

The above evidence points directly to the need for BLACK STUDIES PRO-FESSORS, Black ones, not "Negroes," to establish their own values from inde-pendent field surveys and archaeological excavations whenever necessary. Solely depending upon "GOOD WHITE LIBERAL AFRICANISTS" is totally ridiculous, as it can only add to the further DE-AFRICANIZATION and DE-HUMANIZATION of BLACK PEOPLE everywhere in BLACK STUDIES COURSES set up and operated by said "WHITE LIBERALS." The control of BLACK or AFRICAN STUDIES COURSES and DEPARTMENTS by BLACK-MINDED African-American professors and administrators, alone, can stop the current RACIST attempts to exterminate, CULTURALLY, and sometimes PHYSICALLY, the African-American's heritage of North and East Africa, of which they are entitled because of their African origin. This is an ORIGIN that pre-ceded even the so-called "SEMITIC HYKSOS" about c. 1675, and most definitely the equally "SEMITIC HARIBU" (or "JEWS") that later entered "NEGRO-EGYPT" about c. 1630 from the Asian desert where they were about to become extinct by virtue of "...FAMINE AND PESTILENCE..," according to their own FIRST BOOK OF MOSES (Genesis). All of this supposedly occurred almost two thousand (2000) years before the birth of Jesus Christ - "SUPERSTAR," more than two thousand two hundred and fifty (2250) years before Mohamet ibn Abdullah launched AL'LAH in the Arabian Peninsula at Mecca and the Oasis of Yathrib near Medina (622 C.E. or 1 A.H.).

Just imagine the "WHITE" church and synagogue in the United States of America accepting that the ancient Haribus (today called "Jews") were enslaved

in Africa (Egypt or Kimit) from c. 1630 to c. 1325 B.C.E. under BIG BLACK
NEGRO, or even "NIGGER," slavemasters! Surely you cannot accept this if you
are a "CAUCASIAN" or "SEMITE" (Christian and Jew) of the United States of
America, all of the fifty states and their colonies in the Caribbean Ocean and
the Pacific Ocean that comprise what is commonly called "THE DEMOCRATIC UNION,"
and consider yourself "SUPERIOR" to all of their non-CAUCASIAN, non-SEMITIC,
and/or non-RELIGIOUS brethren of non-WHITE pigment. Why are we over-alarmed
about this revelation? Is it not a fact that the vast majority of European-
American Christians display their hatred for White Jews as much as they do
their so-called "NIGGERS" - the African-Americans (Black Christians, Jews,
Muslims, and all others included)? And, is it not equally a fact that White
Jews do not "LOVE THY..." White Christian "...BROTHER AS THYSELF..." according
to their own Ten Commandments? It seems also, that the only basic LOVE among
European-Americans is the mutual HATRED (Unity) they can muster against their
"...BLACK-SKINNED, THICK LIPS, WOOLLY HAIR, BROAD NOSE..." victims - the
descendants of people Herodotus and other ancient Greeks and Romans described
as the original indigenous inhabitants of North, as well as East, Africa. This
is the only time when there appears to be complete UNITY in 'the house that
George built.' Because of this same reason the truth about the RACIAL-ORIGIN
of Emperor Caracalla and his father - Septimus Severus, also TERTULLIAN, ST.

CYPRIAN, and ST. AUGUSTINE (the latter three were African
"Fathers of the North African Christian Church" -
Christendom in general), cannot be taught. Why? Because
they were "NEGROES," (Blacks); but it must be taught that
they were "CAUCASIANS" or "SEMITES" (White). The fact that
St. Cyprian and Tertullian were indigenous Ethiopians of
Numidia, North Africa, and St. Augustine from Khart Haddas
(Carthage), North Africa, was almost totally suppressed
from even Christians. Most of the few writers that refer to

EMPEROR CARACALLA
father African, mother Syrian
(Murdered A.D. 217)

them as Africans, more often than not (usually) try to show that they were
"...the children of Caucasian North Africans," who they also call "BERBERS,"
or of "ROMAN SOLDIERS LEFT-BACK BY THE ARMIES OF THE LAST PUNIC WAR." In plain

and simple terms - they are presented as having been "WHITE." Most European and European-American style Christian church <u>historians</u> and <u>theologians</u> (Roman Catholic, Protestant, and others) have even suppressed the fact that there were twenty-seven (27) African bishops and several Patriarchs (Popes) in Egypt, where institutionalized Christianity began, before there was the first bishop or Pope in Rome. They prefer to perpetuate the myth about "...ST. PETER..." being "...THE FIRST POPE," and his "...HOLY SEE CENTERED IN ROME." How could <u>"Peter"</u> have been the <u>"First Pope"</u> when, in fact, the Christians of his era were supposedly "...<u>hiding-out in the catacombs of Rome</u>..." because of "...religious persecution" against them by other Romans?* Just as these myths were created, and as Michaelangelo painted his BLOND and BLUE-EYED CAUCASIAN Jesus Christ for the RESSURECTION and LORD'S LAST SUPPER scenes (the twelve disciples also being blonde - not even Judas being able to break the WHITE color-line), equally the "RACIAL SUPERIORITY" of Europeans above all others myth was launched by the forerunners of our 20th century C.E. (A.D.) modern RACISTS and RELIGIOUS BIGOTS. In keeping with the BLOND and BLUE-EYED Nordic God, and God's family, obsession it was necessary to remake Egypt, Ethiopia, Nubia, and all of the other African and Asian nations connected with the origin of the Gods of the so-called "major Western religions" - Jesus Christ and Jehovah - CAUCASIAN and/or SEMITIC; but most of all - free of the slightest evidence of there ever being any "NEGRO" in their background - any BLACKNESS. Thus the "LAMB OF GOD" is proclaimed to be a common "WHITE SHEEP," not the rarest of all sheep - a BLACK SHEEP. This had to be, if the story of Jesus Christ fleeing into a BLACK MAN'S Egypt to find refuge was not to be continued in the King James (British) version of the White Christian HOLY BIBLE; equally if Moses was not to continue being the BLACK Egyptian who "...RECEIVED THE (so-called) TEN COMMANDMENTS FROM JEHOVAH..." for his "CHOSEN PEOPLE ON MOUNT SINAI," in Africa. There could be no BLACK, "NEGRO" or "NEGROID" <u>heritage</u> in any of these stories; not if the first set of books or scriptures (tablets) given to man, according to the story of Moses "RECEIVING THE LAW FROM JEHOVAH,"

---

*See pages **8** and **11** of this work for pictures of BLACK and BLACK-WHITE Romans before the Christians and since. Also see scores of others in F. W. Snowden's <u>BLACKS IN ANTIQUITY: A Greco-Roman Experience</u>.

is to maintain its connection with the White Jews of the United States of
America, Europe, and Israel - fellow members of the so-called "SEMITIC RACE;"
the Black and Brown Jews of Ethiopia (Falashas or Beta Israel), Yemen
(Yemenites) and India (Cochims, etc.) having been relegated to "the Cursed
Children of Canaan."*

The myth of the European and European-American Jews being "...the only
true descendants of the biblical Hebrews..." must be protected at all cost
in White Studies Courses; this is irrespective of what the records say about
the role of the African and Asian Jews, or how many Black Studies Courses there
are going to be in the schools of any type (religious or secular) of learning
in the United States of America. But behind these same myths is the un-spoken
and un-written RACIST GENTLEMEN'S AGREEMENT between White Jews and Christians
who constantly attempt to discredit Herodotus' PHYSICAL (racial) description
of the Ethiopians we have already detailed. Behind it also stands the denial
of one of the oldest groups of Hebrews', the Beta Israel of Ethiopia, East
Africa (also called "FALASHAS"), biological (RACIAL) relationship with the
ancient Haribu (Hebrew, not "Jewish") patriarchs: ...Abraham, Moses, Isaiah
and others, even Jesus Christ - the son of two (2) Jews, Joseph and Mary. Why?
Because the "Falashas" are the BLACKEST of all the Jews in the world; and the
vast majority of them fit the same characteristics Herodotus and other ancients
so aptly used in their description of all of the indigenous peoples of North
and East Africa, (See Herodotus: HISTORIES, Book II, c. 470-450 B.C.E.). But
are the Falashas not "SEMITES" also? Are they not related to SHEM or SEM,
JAPHET, HAM, CANAAN or CHANAAN and KUSH, as well as MIZRAIR (Egypt)? If not;
who removed them from ADAM'S and EVE'S family-tree, and when?

The professional SEMITE and CAUCASIAN must also be a professional NEGRO-
PHOBIST. He, or she, must stick to the "SEMITIC NOSE," "WHITE SKIN," and
"NORDIC FEATURES" in order to maintain the myth that such RACISM is synonymous
with the teaching of the "...HOLY INSPIRED WRITINGS OF (White) MEN OF GOD."
If this is not done, there goes the major premise of the PURE WHITE GOD and

---

*This myth has been properly treated elsewhere in this work. See AFRICAN
ORIGINS OF THE MAJOR "WESTERN RELIGIONS;" also AFRICA: MOTHER OF "WESTERN
CIVILIZATION;" both by Yosef ben-Jochannan for further detailed analysis of
this myth.

HEAVEN myth that has kept White America (Christians, Jews, and others) going for the past 400 or more years. To a much greater degree it has also kept "Western (White) Civilization" (Western Europe, Great Britain and European-America) in the same mirage for a few hundred years longer. "WESTERN CIVILIZA-TION" (whatever these two words mean), in this sense, does not in any-way shape-or-form include ancient Greece or Rome; the ancient Romans and Greeks never being aware of the type of RACISM and RELIGIOUS BIGOTRY without which modern Europeans and European-Americans believe they cannot survive. This does not mean that many of the ancients did not take note of the varied complexities of their physical person and the pigment of their skin. To the contrary, the fact is that they frequently recorded those differences for various reasons.

The myth of a "SEMITIC NORTH AFRICA" that was exclusive of "Negroes"(or "Ethiopians") had other basic origins, the most dangerous of them being the RACIST proclamation in the FIRST and SECOND (Genesis and Exodus) BOOKS OF MOSES, otherwise two/fifths part of the entire HOLY TORAH ("Old Testament") is based upon a North African EXPERIENCE. For example: In the FIRST BOOK OF MOSES one of the wicked and most SINFUL things the Hebrew (Jewish) God - Jehovah - did was to condemn a whole RACE of people; thus the following from Genesis IX, 18-27 of the Hebrew HOLY TORAH as presented in the OLD TESTAMENT OF THE HOLY BIBLE (Confraternity Version):

> The sons of Noe (Noah) who went out of the ark were Sen (Shem), Ham[25] and Japheth. These three were the sons of Noe and from these the whole earth was peopled. Now Noe began to till the soil, and he planted a vineyard. When he drank of the wine, he bacame drunk and lay naked in his tent. Ham saw his father's nakedness and told his two brothers outside. But Sen and Japheth took a robe, and laying it upon their shoulders, went backward and covered their father's nakedness; as their faces were turned away, they did not see their father's nakedness. When Noe awoke from his drunkedness and learned what his youngest son had done to him, he said; "Cursed be Canaan; meanest of slaves shall be to his brethren." Then he said: Blessed be the Lord, the God of Sem; let Chanaan be his slave. May God expand Japheth; let him dwell in the tents of Sem; let Chanaan be his slave."

The above story takes on many interpretations, the most dangerous being that which Jehovah (the Jewish or Semitic God) supposedly branded African people (Ethiopians or "Negroes," Blacks) as "CHANAANITES;" thus SLAVES TO THE SEMITES - "the children of Ham being slaves to the children of Sem." To make this little it of RELIGIOUS BIGOTRY and JEWISH RACISM against African (Black) people

("NEGROES") be that more explicit, we find sixth (6th) century C.E. Babylonian

Talmudist "scholars" of European Jewish ghettos writing the following:

> Now I cannot beget the fourth son whose children I
> would have ordered to serve you and your brothers!
> Therefore it must be Canaan, your first born, whom
> they enslave. And since you have disabled me...doing
> ugly things in blackness of night, Canaan's children
> shall be born ugly and black! Moreover, because you
> twisted your head around to see my nakedness, your
> grandchildren's hair shall be twisted into kinks,
> and their eyes red; again because your lips jested
> at my misfortune, theirs shall swell; and because
> you neglected my nakedness, they shall go naked,
> and <u>their male members shall be shamefully elon-
> gated! Men of this race are called Negroes, their
> forefather Canaan commanded them to love theft and
> fornication, to be banded together in hatred of
> their masters and never to tell the truth.</u>

The above quotation is taken from R. Graves and R. Patti's HEBREW MYTHS,

New York, 1964, p. 121. On page 23 of the OLD TESTAMENT of the HOLY BIBLE

(Confraternity Version), Guild Press, New York (1952, 1955, 1961), the com-

mentator Rev. Joseph Grispino, S.M., S.S.L., was moved to write the following

about the type of RACIST interpretation above by Jewish Talmudists, the only

difference being that he was addressing his remarks to European and European-

American (Caucasian or White) "Christian" Racist of today, whereas the Tal-

mudists were addressing other professional SEMITES of their day. Rev. Joseph

Grispino gave his own comments in the footnotes of the page. He wrote:

> ...The tenth century writer wants to exhort the Israelites
> to avoid the lewd practices of the Chanaanite neighbors.
> Now the Israelites thought that every happening, e.g.,
> their conquest of the Chanaanites, came about because
> God wanted it to happen from all eternity. To dramatize
> this the writer makes God bless the ancestor of his
> race, Sem, and curse the ancestor of Chanaan, Ham. This
> story does not say that the Negroes or the Africans are
> the slaves of the white men. To use this story as an
> argument from Scripture to uphold Apartheid or a
> segregationist policy is to interpret the text against the
> mind of the writer.

The Reverend should have lived among the 6th century professional Jewish

"SEMITES" of the Babylonian Talmudist school in the ghettos of Europe when they

were getting ready to write their own SEMITIC RACISM and BIGOTED RELIGIOUS

dogma. He could have told them what they were about to establish by such

RACISM the <u>Calvinists</u> of South Africa and the White Nationalists of the United

States of America were going to adopt as their basic creed - à-la-NEGROPHOBISM.
But there is something else much more important in the Reverend's citation I
should have dealt with, the word in the Hebrew language during the biblical
writers lifetime which was, supposedly, synonymous with the modern term -
"NEGRO," in order to assume that the "CURSE" Noah (or Noe) placed upon his
grandson Canaan.or Chanaan (through Jehovah's power), was the color of the
African's skin - "BLACK?" And, why should a "CURSE" from Noah mean much more
than a "CURSE" from Noah's Semitic God - Jehovah? The proof! We see Jehovah
CURSING His own "GROUND" He created before Noah was born, according to Genesis
5, 28-31. The myth follows that...:

> When Lamech was one hundred and eighty-two years old,
> he became the father of a son, and called him Noah,
> saying, "This one shall bring us comfort from our
> work and from the toil of our hands in the ground
> which the Lord cursed." Lamech lived five hundred
> and ninety-five years after the birth of Noah, and
> had other sons and daughters.

In the same Book of Genesis Jehovah is seen CURSING, KILLING, COMMITING
GENOCIDE, and doing all manner of things which HE has forbidden mere mortals
to do. In everyone of the Five Books of Moses, EXODUS in particular, Jehovah
sanctions "SLAVERY" for multitudes of people and their nations; but he totally
abhored it with respect to His "CHOSEN" Jews that "STOPPED AND PURCHASED SLAVES
ON THEIR WAY OUT OF EGYPT..." with money and jewelry which they had embezzled
from their fellow-Egyptians who worshipped God, RA; all with the help of God -
Jehovah.

A second look at GENESIS and EXODUS will be very good at this juncture.
For if the writers of Genesis and Exodus, who wrote these stories long after
Moses had suddenly disappeared from Mount Sinai (just as speedily as he had appeared with the turn of the last page of Genesis to the first page of Exodus),
had taken time to check what they were writing, with respect to their own
RACISM and RELIGIOUS BIGOTRY, probably we would have had a totally different
set of mythological stories - "God inspired writings" (or "Scriptures") no
doubt.

With respect to the labeling of CHANAAN (Canaan) of HAM (Chanaan's father)
"BLACK" the Hebrew word "KEMI" was used in the place where color was inserted

by the modern "SEMITICISTS." However, the word "KEMI," literally, meant "EGYPT" in biblical Hebrew. And by no stretch of the imagination could it be interpreted to mean "BLACK," worse yet "NEGRO," unless by sick minds. (See Genesis x:6, Psalms cv:23 and cvi:22). Of course this RACIST story, allegedly "WRITTEN BY MOSES" and other "JEHOVAH" (God) - "INSPIRED MEN," no "INSPIRED" women of course, had to be Europeanized by Torahdic and Talmudic "scholars" of the 6th century C.E.; people who were themselves suffering from the effects of CAUCASIAN "RACISM" almost as much as the "BLACKS" or "NEGROES" they were making the target for further persecution and possible genocide. For, in those days, all over Europe and Great Britain, "SEMITICISM" (or "SEMITISM") was the "MARK" or "CURSE" (scourge) of the ancestors of those who now prostelize it as the panecea for being a kosher North African; its zenith or claim to fame being manifested in the "SEMITIC NORTH AFRICA" syndrome of the 20th century C.E. professional "SEMITIC" writers and "EDUCATORS," many of them dominate "BLACK" and "AFRICAN STUDIES" Departments.

It is to be expected that my former religious associates, many of those with whom I have followed the teachings and practice of ancient Hebrewism (called "Judaism" as a misnomer today), including the BIGOTED custom of praying for a brother or sister as if "DEAD" because he or she "...married a non-Jew" (male or female). But, my former associates have selected to remain in the "ISRAELITE" nation in face of seeing what the RACIST myth of "THE CHOSEN PEOPLE" idiosyncrasy has done to themselves and the overall African people. They may even join hands with other "CHOSEN PEOPLE" in making me the worse ANTI-SEMITE next to Adolph Hitler. But, this will not make them any closer to the "BLACK REVOLUTION," which they should have been in the vanguard fighting. For it is not because of their "JEWISHNESS," or their "CHOSEN PEOPLE" status, that they too are suffering at the hands of the "CAUCASIANISTS, HAMITICISTS" and "SEMITICISTS;" it is primarily because of the BLACK COLOR we all share with our equally BLACK sisters and brothers of every religion in which BLACK people hold membership. This of course could, and would, be used by many of them to try and solidify their "INTEGRATION" with the "SEMITICISTS" so many have so long desired, and labored for, over the past forty (40) or more years.

Never-the-less I, as a former worshiper of the God - JEHOVAH (the God of the ancient Ethiopians of the Haribu faith), cannot ignore the RACIST actions and RELIGIOUS BIGOTRY of White or Black Jews, White or Black Christians, White or Black Muslims, in their bastardization and plagiarization of the history and heritage of my "MOTHER-CONTINENT" - Alkebu-lan.[26]

The almost frightening quietness of the "BLACK ISRAELITES" in the United States of America, very much unlike their BLACK Muslim and BLACK Christian Nationalist brothers and sisters (not to mention all of those Africans who practice religions Christian, Jews, and Muslims call "ANIMISTIC" and "HEATHEN"); in light of the attempted genocide against BLACK peoples everywhere, culturally and physically, which has been, and is still being done by those who command the "POWER STRUCTURE" (both Christian and Jew), is CRIMINAL. But, there is no doubt that these African Hebrew people will also have to join other Africans who do not share their religious belief, in order to protect our ancient North African ancestors' history and heritage from the plagiarous attacks by professional "SEMITICISTS, HAMITICISTS" and "CAUCASIANISTS;" all of whom operate under the disguise of being "LIBERAL WHITE AFRICANISTS" and "AUTHORITIES ON AFRICA." These "educators," most of whom bar BLACK "scholars" who differ with their plagiarized versions of North and East Africa's history and High-Culture in particular, the rest of Africa generally, also control what BLACK students read and think. Therefore, who else can best make this confrontation meaningfull than those on the inside of the nation, ISRAEL, and those who were once in? Who else among the BLACKS can deal with the history of the Jews and their encounter with fellow Ethiopians (Africans, etc.) that gave them FREEDOM and HAVEN (food, clothing, shelter and protection) following their aimless wandering around the Eur-Asian (today's Middle East) desert with nothing but a few shepherds and their herds? Who else should remind people that the Book of Genesis (First Book of Moses) is as much a BLACK MAN'S history as it is any other person; and that Egypt, where much of its experience took place, is still in a BLACK MAN'S country? Who else should deal face-to-face with European and European-American Jews, as well as Christians, who make it their business to commit cultural genocide against BLACK people in most "AFRICAN" and "BLACK STUDIES" Courses (many of whom bar "BLACK" professors from "AFRICAN STUDIES"

Departments), and not subject to be charged with the usual "ANTI-SEMITISM"?
The Black Israelites should. They can do this from the same position that so
many other non-Jews must otherwise treat with the greatest of care. Unless
those of us who continue to call ourselves "BLACK ISRAELITES," or those of us
who once carried this name, are ready to face-up to this question (our sacred
responsibility to our own BLACK selves), we do not have any RIGHT whatsoever
to expect that other religiously identified segments of BLACK-AMERICAN or
BLACK-CARIBBEAN people, and of course AFRICANS, should follow our lead in any
manner of endeavour - including the way to JEHOVAH. The longer BLACK ISRAELITES
sit idly-by and continue to straddle the political, social, economic and
religious fence in WHITE <u>Christian</u> and <u>Jewish</u> United States of America, waiting
to see in which direction the RACIAL ball will fall before we rush to the
victors' side, the more we contribute to the professional "SEMITES" syndrome
of an "INDIGENOUS SEMITIC NORTH AFRICA" that was "CAUCASIAN" or "INDO (Asian)-
EUROPEAN ARYAN." A NORTH AFRICA which, supposedly, had its beginning at some-
place called "THE GARDEN OF EDEN," around the Tigris and Eurphrates rivers in
southwestern Asia; there being no "GARDEN," muchless "EDEN," at the foot
of the CAUCASUS mountains. Of course, in this "GARDEN OF EDEN" there were also
"NEGROE SLAVES FOR THE SEMITES." "SLAVES" whom their God, Jehovah, allegedly,
made on the command of a "CURSE" issued by Noe (Noah) against his son's (Ham)
children - the Canaanites.

<u>REFLECTIONS</u>

As we look back on the good old Sahara (which European and European-
American historians and other <u>"educators"</u> treat as if it was, or is, a myth-
ically <u>mysterious impassable ocean</u>)     <u>"gateway"</u> now, just as it was in ancient
times to all of Africa's sons and daughters to its South and to its North, we
find the following: First it was the main <u>"passageway"</u> for the African suppliers
of gold to Europe. They came from places as far off as Nigeria (Benin Kingdom)
up until the so-called "Middle Ages." It was also used as the land where people
of various language-groups and cultural distinction of Africa met with many of
Asia and Europe. All of this cross-cultural intercourse began thousands of years
before the arrival of Islam and its Arabian <u>jihadists</u> in North Africa during

1640 C.E.[27] Yet, we can still read where some "SEMITE" or the other of our mid-twentieth century recently published a book, claiming that "SEMITIC (Jewish) PEOPLES" called "ALMORAVIDS" (Almohades) "WERE THE ONES WHO ESTABLISHED THE WEST AFRICAN EMPIRE OF GHANA IN 300 A.D." And, "THEY WERE WHITE, BUT THE NATIVES WERE NEGROES." This type of "SEMITIC" racism could be best understood, but not tolerated, when one read's it in Robin Hallett's revised work of the 1958 edition of E. W. Bovill's THE GOLDEN TRADE OF THE MOORS, which Bovill had produced as a revised version of his own book - CARAVANS OF OLD SAHARA (1933). This book by Hallett is truly unpalatable by any standard; especially when one observes that many so-called "African historians" regurgitate the same RACIST teaching in AFRICAN and BLACK Studies Courses as a direct result of reading it. Yet, one is reminded that a Europeanized or European-Americanized (Whitened) African or African-American, one who represents the zenith of what was truly called an "UNCLE TOM" (house or field), will do and say anything his cultural slavemasters desire of him (or her). The best example of this type of NIGGARDLY act by a noted "NIGGAR"* appears at the ending of a book written by one Carl Christian Reindorf, allegedly a Gold Coast (presently part of the Republic of Ghana, West Africa) African, in 1895 C.E., which he named HISTORY OF THE GOLD COAST AND ASANTE. It is a work that continues to enjoy being quoted by countless European and European-American "AFRICANISTS" as one of the best "AUTHORITATIVE SOURCE OF AFRICAN HISTORY AND CULTURE." The good brother, obviously Europeanized and Christianized À-LA-EUROPEAN STYLE to the pulp of his teeth, wrote the following in high praises of his slavemasters' and their homeland:

> Rule, supreme rule, Britania, rule,
> Thy newly acquired colony on the Gold Coast!...
> Two mighty foes impede her way,
> Ignorance and blood-stained superstition.
> To rule and not to fight such deadly foes,
> Is not Britain's way....

As we begin to condemn this unfortunate African brother who has had his total person, worse of all his mind, de-Africanized, and then Europeanized (brainwashed), but mostly Anglo-Saxonized, we must be ready to note that all

---

*Take special notation of the use of this very common English word and do not confuse it with its European-American corruption - "NIGGER."

of us who answer to the name "AFRICAN PEOPLE," for the most part, had been

equally denuded of our basic humanity at one time or another under the control

of the same type of "Western" slavemasters, who showed their worse venom during

the dastardly SLAVE TRADE and its PLANTATION SYSTEM, each being first in-

stituted by the Spanish nation (Spain) under Queen Isabella and King Ferdinand

upon the advice of the Holy Roman Catholic See of Pope Martin Vᵗʰ Emissary -

The Rt. Rev. Bishop Bartolome de Las Casas - on the Island of Hispaniola

(formerly Hayte, today's Haiti) in the year c. 1503 or c. 1506 C.E. (A.D.).[28]

As we return to the "CAUCASIANISTS" and "SEMITICISTS" of Europe, Britain,

and European-America, and their removal of their "NEGROES" from many parts of

Africa, we find Walter B. Emery writing the following in his book, EGYPT IN

NUBIA, page 157 (allegedly quoting from a stele about a BLACK pharaoh of Egypt,

Semuret III, victory over a BLACK Nubian pharaoh):*

> ...Valiance is eagerness, cowardice is to slink back;
> he is truly a craven who is repelled upon his border;
> since the Negro harkens to the ? of the mouth; it is
> answering him which drives him back; when one is
> eager against him, he turns his back; when he slinks
> back, he begins to be eager.

The above was taken from the tenth (10ᵗʰ) to fourteenth (14ᵗʰ) lines of the

quotation. On page 158 Emery also engaged in his own bit of RACISM with respect

to the term "NEGRO;" a word which he added to the vocabulary of Pharaoh

Senusret II in his remarks about the Nubians' cowardice. Emery wrote:

> The reference to Egypt's enemies as 'Negroes' is
> misleading, for the people of Kush were not Negroes
> as we understand the term as applied to this racial
> group today. The Egyptians used the term 'Negro'
> (nhsi) to designate all the dark-skinned people of
> the south, whatever their race.

Here, again, we witness the total confusion in which European-American RACISTS

operate with respect to their own COLOR PREJUDICE line they have established

for North Africa and Nile Valley High-Cultures (civilizations). The impression

this "LIBERAL AFRICANIST" tries to give apparently, is that the Egyptians were

---

*Is it coincidental that "Western" historians always omit the name of the
Pharaohs of Nubia in their writings between Egypt and other Nile Valley nations.?
Note that the same common practice applies to biblical Hebrew characters and
Egyptian pharaohs in reverse. For example: "Moses," the Hebrew hero of the
Book of Exodus, has a name; but the Egyptian hero of the same Book is only
called "Pharaoh" - which means King, President, Emperor, head of state, etc.

not "DARK-SKINNED PEOPLE..." as other Africans south of Egypt. Certainly very few ancient historians could have been obliged to concede that the Egyptians were "...DARK-SKINNED PEOPLE." Even the most honored of the "CAUCASIAN" and "SEMITIC" North and East Africa mythologists, M. D. W. Jeffries, also agreed to this fact  But C. G. Seligman, another of the world-renown HAMITICISTS, the author of RACES OF AFRICA, stated that they were "...DARK-SKINNED HAMITES FROM EUROPE... Secondly: the word "(nhsi)" by no stretch of ones imagination, except that of Emery's and his school of "educators," stood for the corrupted genocidal term created by the Portuguese, "NEGRO;" nor for anything whatsoever resembling it. Why is this true? Because the Egyptians were not aware of this term in their vocabulary; and they enjoyed quite an extensive one.

Another point to be raised is; why was "KUSH" even mentioned? The entire alleged quotation, in its present form, dealt with "Nubia" and the "Nubians." Next; most of the professional Semitic and Caucasian "EGYPTOLOGISTS" (as they call themselves, have already concluded that "THE NUBIANS WERE NEGROES." And there is hardly any book written by a "WHITE LIBERAL" historian which does not recite this alleged "FACT." Thus, there is no need for further bibliographical notation on this point. Thus, one wonders if Emery has ever seen and read Herodotus', Eusbius', Josephus', Statius', Philostratus', Diodorus', Lucretius', and other Romans and Greeks , works of antiquity in terms of their DESCRIPTION OF THE PHYSICAL APPEARANCE AND COLOR OF THE EGYPTIANS, NUBIANS, KUSHITES, AND OTHER ETHIOPIANS (Blacks, "Negroes," etc.) OF THE ENTIRE NILE VALLEYS (Blue and White) AND NORTH AFRICA. Based upon the wealth of evidence these men left in their writings, and the fact that he demonstrated no knowledge of same, he, obviously, did not. Where, and in what work, could Emery say that he witnessed one solitary reference to the Africans of ancient times other than "ETHIOPIANS," "BLACKS," or nationals of individual African nations - "Nubians, Egyptians," etc.? If this "EGYPTOLOGIST," and all the others like him, is not aware of said African peoples description, both physically and color, it is suggested that he read the following works: IMAGINES, 1.29; IMAGINES, 1.7; Plautus, POENULUS, 1113 (where he wrote that they were "Black Men Baked By The Sun" - "Ore atque oculis pernigris")' Agatharchide, DE MARI ERYTHRAEO

58 Geographi Graeci Minores; Lucretius 6.722, 6.1109; J. H. Lewis, THE BIOLOGY OF THE NEGRO[29] (Chicago, 1942);* Diodorus 3,29.1; and Statius, THEBAIS 5.427-428. Not one of the above men wrote anything in their works which could have been conscruded to be "NEGROID PHYSICAL TRAITS!" Such a depiction was alien to their culture and time. The ancient Greeks and Romans who lived, worked, and studied under the Egyptians and other Nile Valley Ethiopians (Blacks, "Negroes," or Africans), at that period in history, referred to everyone from the continent of Africa as "Ethiopians." Why? Because the vast majority of them fell within the general physical and color characteristics already mentioned, which were given by all of the above writers named. Diodorus, for example, wrote that:

> "...the majority of Ethiopians" (AFRICANS)** "that dwell along the Nile[31] are black-skinned, flat-nosed, and woolly-haired...," etc.

The next point to be considered in the "SEMITIC" syndrome is; at what point, geographically, did ancient Nubia end with respect to ancient Egypt? Did not the Nubians and Egyptians share the same language and Gods, and jointly built temples and pyramids to their Gods? And, who decided that Nubia, geographically that is, "began at the Second Cataract?"; its northernmost border. What documentation was submitted to substantiate this latter conclusion? The fact is that the ancient indigenous Egyptians and Nubians did not establish any set delineation (boundary line) or geographic demarcation with respect to any of the Six Cataracts of the Nile River; nor did they do so for political or social reasons. The theory of 'Nubia beginning at the Second Cataract' is typical of so many other myths about the Nile Valley nations concocted by "Western EDUCATORS." The political jingoism that is always demonstrated by Europeans and European-Americans with regards to Nubia's and Egypt's alleged geo-political boundaries is nothing more or less than the direct result of the common SEMITICISTS and CAUCASIANISTS mental illusion in European-American educational institutions. For at no time in ancient African history, or prehistory, was there in existence any barrier to the indigenous Nile Valley (Blue or White) people's amalgamation on the basis of physical appearance -

---

*Listed, but not an ancient work. A very good reference for contrast.
**Inserted by your author for the sake of clarity only.

THICK LIPS, BROAD NOSE, WOOLLY HAIR (RACE) or COLOR OF SKIN (BLACK).* As to the "boundaries," if in fact there was any established, and no proof seems to be in existence for such a position on a geographical basis, not one was ever charted. However, each conquering monarch (pharaoh) of both sides established his own imaginary boundary line to the extent he felt his military power existed. When the Egyptians were the victors the line went southwards. It went drastically. in the opposite direction when the Nubians or Kushites were the victors - sometimes all the way to the Kimit[32] (Mediterranean) Sea.

## RACE AS A FACTOR IN EGYPT???

If it is the "POINTED NOSE"* of many of the pharaohs that made them become "SEMITES" in the mind of the Semiticists; then Africans all over the continent of Alkebu-lan (Africa) must be fitted into this category. Millions of the indigenous African people of Kenya, Ethiopia, Congo, Guinea, Mauritania and Tanganyika, only to name a few, satisfy this description. But, what about the pharaohs who had "FLAT NOSE," those of whom we do not find very often in books written by "SEMITIC" or "CAUCASIAN" (White; Christian, Jewish, Muslim, etc.) educators of every discipline dealing with Africa and things-African? (See pp. 8 , 24 , & 66 of this work for visual proof of the "FLAT-NOSED" type).

Is it the HAIR? Note that most of the ROYAL EGYPTIANS, as did the royalty of Nubia, Kush (Ethiopia), Puanit (Punt - the areas of Kenya and Somalia) and the Great Lakes northern regions (Uganda, Eastern Congo, Tanganyika, Burundi, Urundi, etc.), wore WIGS. Also, that the PEPPER-AND-CORN (woolly)** formation of the hair shown in Egyptian pictures, and on artifacts of other nations, was very common among all of the national groupings of the Nile Valley High-Cultures. This was equally true for the Ethiopians (Egyptians, Nubians, Kushites, Libyans, Khart Haddans or "Carthaginians," and others from parts South of the Sahara) who resided in ancient Greece and Rome, many of whom were of the UPPER-CLASS in each country. These facts can be best observed from a pictorial basis in Frank M. Snowden's book, BLACKS IN ANTIQUITY: Ethiopians in the Greco-

---

*Do not overlook the fact that there were thousands who had "THIN LIPS, NARROW NOSE, STRAIGHT HAIR, AND LIGHT OF SKIN.
**Take note of this observation with respect to thousands of the ancient Greeks and Romans shown on pages 8 , 11 and 24 of this work.

Roman Experience.[33]

The color of the ancient Egyptians has been conceded by most SEMITICISTS
and CAUCASIANISTS to have been "BLACK;" by others, at least, "DARK-SKINNED."
Of course "DARK-SKINNED" is no more a color than "NEGRO" or "COLOURED" is.
However, the Egyptians "BLACKNESS" is steadily becoming WHITER and WHITER as
each SEMITICIST or CAUCASIANIST try to out-do the other in proving the
"RACIAL PURITY" of his or her allegedly "SEMITIC," or "CAUCASIAN," Egyptian
ancestor's antiquity in Africa.

Why did the Egyptians take very articulate care to show that their Asian
(the so-called "SEMITIC") captives (SLAVES) in the paintings on the walls of
their pyramids, and on papyri, had exceptionally protruding nose; which was
very much unlike themselves?[34] Why did the Egyptians not treat their Asian
captives ("Semites, Hamites, Caucasians" and "Indo-European Aryans") with
greater humanity than they allegedly treated their Nubian ("NEGRO") captives?
Because the ancient Egyptians, people like those one could have met on the
streets of Nubia and Kush, or in the Harlems of the United States of America,
made every effort to show that their Asian captives (SLAVES) were, in fact,
very different physically, in color, culturally, religiously, and otherwise,
than themselves. At no time before the so-called "Semitic Hyksos" invasion
of Egypt (c. 1675 B.C.E.) did the Egyptians even consider it necessary to
make any distinction between themselves and other Africans (Ethiopians),
except as it referred to the Gods. Yet, it was only to those Gods which they
did not equally share with other Nile Valley Africans (BLACKS).[35] And, we have
seen that most of the Gods of Nubia and Kush were worshipped by the Egyptians.
Also, that most of them originated from further SOUTH - in Puanit (Punt, today's
Somaliland, Kenya, and Afras).

Just as there was no geographic or social barrier between the people of
the Nile (Blue and White) Valleys; equally there was no major difference whatsoever between the family structure of the Egyptians and any of the other
African nations of antiquity along the Nile and Great Lakes. This is not the
way professor George Posener of the College de France sees it; nor his two
assistants, Serge Sauneron and Jean Yoyotte, that collaborated with him on his

40

book, DICTIONARY OF EGYPTIAN CIVILIZATION.[36] On pages 85 and 86 they stated that the Egyptian family of ancient times was similar to that of each and every twentieth (20th) century C.E. European. Also, that:

>...there was nothing of primitive Africa about it, nothing g
>that foreshadows Islam.

Is it not much more logical that an ancient Egyptian family's LIFE-STYLE would have been closer to his fellow Africans' elsewhere on the African continent, during like period of time, than with twentieth (20th) century C.E. European or European-American families? Not according to our two modern CAUCASIAN-ISTS who, like their fellow SEMITICISTS, see everything Egyptian minus their "NEGRO" involvement. But, is this not another way of implying that they ancient indigenous Africans of Egypt were closer in CULTURE and RACE (physical characteristics) to Europeans and European-Americans - including so-called "SEMITES" and "CAUCASIANS," and even "INDO-EUROPEAN ARYANS", in Europe than they were with their own African brothers and sisters who shared control over the same area of Africa intermitently? Did these men, "SCHOLARS" and "LIBERAL WHITE AFRICANISTS" I would suppose, not know that the indigenous Africans and their High-Cultures (civilizations) of the Nile Valleys (Blue and White, the Atbara River included) also migrated from the SOUTH to the NORTH, and not in the opposite direction as was once taught by most European and European-American "EDUCATORS"? That, even the GODS the ancient Egyptians worshipped, they said "...WERE BROUGHT TO KIMIT" (Egypt or Sais) "BY SOUTHERNERS..." who came from as far off SOUTH as the Empire of Monomotapa[37] and the High-Cultures of "the great" Zimbabwe, Dhlo-Dhlo, and other Rowzis areas - these places being many of the areas where the oldest known "MAN-LIKE APES"and/or "APE-LIKE MEN" (fossils) as Zinjanthropus boisie, Boskop Man, Zimbabwe (so-called "Rhodesia") Man, and many others, have been unearthed within the last two (2) generations in the modern "GARDEN OF EDEN" (central East Africa)? Dr. Albert Churchward made these facts very clear in his many books; the best on this particular subject being one entitled, SIGNS AND SYMBOLS OF PRIMORDIAL MAN, which he published in London, 1920. In this work he cited that the so-called "NEGRO," or as he called them - "TRUE NEGRO, MASABA NEGRO" and "NILOTIC NEGRO," also the "PYGMIES" (correctly TWA people according to their own language), were the MOTHERS and FATHERS of Africa's High-Cultures, Egypt being no exception to this fact. Dr. Churchward also cited that all of mankind (Caucasians, Semites, Hamites, and Indo-European Aryans, included) originated from the same "NEGROES" and "PYGMIES." Dr. Churchward's PALAEONTOLOGICAL MAP, which he called "PREHISTORIC AFRICA," in another of his work further elaborated on this aspect of Africa's prehistory and mankind's beginning in the African "...GARDEN OF EDEN...." (See map below).

## PREHISTORIC AFRICA

From Albert Churchward, M.D. (British archaeologist and palaeontologist of world fame), ORIGIN AND EVOLUTION OF FREEMASONRY. Dr. Churchward stated that the area marked "HOME OF THE PYGMIES" was the "...ORIGINAL HOME OF MAN;" completely refuting Professor M.D.W. Jeffreys' and Dr. Donald Weidner's NEGROPHOBIA. Is it not strange that the "AUTHORITIES" are so far apart on whether or not the indigenous Africans settled over their entire continent as Europeans and Asians did on theirs?

Count C.F. Volney in his book, RUINS OF EMPIRE (Paris, c. 1800 C.E.), also

pointed-out that "SABLED-SKINNED AFRICANS" (called "Negroes" today) "DESIGNED
AND BUILT THE PYRAMIDS OF EGYPT..." and "CREATED THE CIVILIZATION..." (High-
Culture) known as "Pharonic Egypt" or "Dynastic Egypt." His very close friend, Ba-
ron Viviant Denon's book, TRAVELS IN EGYPT AND SYRIA, was also written in the
latter part of the eighteenth (18th) century C.E. In it Baron Denon was very
emphatic that "...AN OFFICER OF NAPOLEON'S(Boneparte) ARMY..." had his men
"...BLAST THE NOSE AND LIPS OF THE GREAT SPHINX OF GIZEH ASSUNDER WITH CANNON-
FIRE..." because they could not bear to stand and look at its "...NEGRO APPEAR-
ANCE...." Strange it is that twentieth century C. E. CAUCASIANS and SEMITES
would prefer that we forget these first-hand reports and documentation from
their fellow Europeans who visited the scene, but prefer to accept their own
wishful illusion with respect to their "CHOSEN PEOPLE" status. The idea of a
"NEGRO-LESS" North Africa, or East of the Sahara, with a line of BLACK demarcation drawn around "NEGRO NUBIA," is one which ignores the fact that the so-
called "INDO-EUROPEAN CAUCASIAN ARYANS" or "SEMITES" did not appear NORTH OF
THE SAHARA, nor EAST of it, before the Asian-Hyksos invasion of Egypt in c. 1675
B.C.E., the Asian-Assyrian in vasion of c. 663 B.C.E., and the Asian-Persian invasion of c. 525 B.C.E.; also the European-Greek invasion of c. 332 B.C.E., and
European-Roman invasion of c. 149 B.C.E.;* and finally the invasion by so-
called "Asian-HAMITES" from the Arabian Peninsula in c. 640 C.E. or A.D. (the year
18 A.H. of the Muslim Calendar). If such be the case, and this is what history
has so far revealed; when, and how, did NORTH or EAST Africa became indigenous-
ly "SEMITIC, HAMITIC," or "CAUCASIAN," even "CAUCASOID"?

RELIGION AS THE

In the area of RELIGION the ancient indigenous Africans of Egypt took very
strict precautions in painting things pertaining to DEATH in WHITE; but, for
LIFE they used BLACK, BROWN, and YELLOW, lavishly. This tradition we have seem
in the many DEATH scenes in the BOOK OF THE DEAD and PAPYRUS OF ANI, where the
KAA (Ka) bird (the Spirit of the Life) is in a BROWNISH-BLACK, but the BAA (Ba)
bird (the Spirit of the Death) is in a very BRIGHT-WHITE. Ani (the deceased) and
his wife are presented this way throughout the PAPYRUS OF ANI. If the Egyptians

*c. 149 B.C.E. - Invasion of Khart Haddas (Carthage). c. 47 or 30 B.C.E. = In-
vasion of Kimit (Egypt) under the Ptolemies reign.

were WHITE, as most of the modern SEMITICISTS have been trying to prove over the past one hundred and fifty (150) years, equally the CAUCASIANISTS and HAMITICISTS; why did they use WHITE as the colour that represented SHAME, SORROW, DEATH, MOURNING, etc.? And, since we are to believe that this branch of the indigenous African people was very similar in LIFE-STYLE to modern Europeans and European-Americans, but not in anyway or fashion to "AFRICANS SOUTH OF THE SAHARA" and the "WESTERN WORLD" ("Negroes"), educators expounding this myth should also explain why modern AFRICANS SOUTH OF THE SAHARA always hold to the ancient polygamous marriage-pattern commonly practised by their ancient Nile Valley and Great Lakes region brothers and sisters of thousands of years - those of Kimit (Egypt), Nubia and Kush in particular. They should also explain why this tradition has been abondoned by Europeans and European-Americans, if ever they had it, as "ANTI-SOCIAL"? And, why do European and European-American[38] colonialists and "Christian" missionaries try to stomp out such practices in Africa and other areas of the entire world where African peoples have continued this aspect of ancient African LIFE-STYLE? Is there any records available which show that the AFRICANS SOUTH OF THE SAHARA ever abondoned this aspect of their High-Culture?

GENOCIDE AND EUROPEAN-STYLE CHRISTIANITY

The role of GENOCIDE in European-American style "Christianity," which Europeans and European-Americans under the name "MISSIONARIES" engaged in against the indigenous Africans in their own continent, Africa, and against the Africans own religions (many of them being the foundation of Judaism, Christianity and Islam), can be best observed in professor C.P. Groves' four (4) volumes work, THE PLANTING OF CHRISTIANITY IN AFRICA.[39] His type of "CHRISTIANITY" was used by European and European-American colonialists and imperialists (SEMITES AND CAUCASIANS) at the Berlin Conference On West African Trade..., etc. of 1884-85 C.E. and the Brussels Conference (the extension of the former) of 1886-96 C.E.[40] under the pretext of "...STOPPING THE ARAB SLAVE TRADE IN AFRICA" and "...BRINGING CIVILIZATION AND CHRISTIANITY TO THE UNCIVILIZED AND HEATHEN NATIVES...," etc. The word "NATIVE" was, and still is, used as the 'FAMILY NAME' of each and every African. Yet, Ethiopia was a "CHRISTIAN NATION" more than one hundred and twenty (120) years before Rome (the first European

44

"Christian" nation). North Africa produced the most noted of the "CHRISTIAN CHURCH FATHERS" of Christendom - Tertullian, St. Cyprian and St. Augustine; this the arch perpetrators of RACISM and RELIGIOUS BIGOTRY in European-American style "CHRISTIANITY" carefully overlooked. Conveniently, they also forgot that it was three (3) indigenous African (BLACK) women who were "...THE FIRST CHRISTIAN MARTYRS" in all of Christendom. Yet these BLACK women and men appear in all sorts of religious paintings in every aspect very similar to the WHITE CAUCASIAN ARYAN and BLOND BLUE-EYED Jesus Christ of Michaelangelo's CRUCIFIXION and LAST SUPPER.

The above may not mean very much to those of us who may be professing Islam at this period in our cultural revolutionary involvement. For many of us believe that jumping from a Jewish-Semite or Christian-Caucasian "BAG" of the "SE-METICISTS" and "CAUCASIANISTS" to the heavenly dream world of Islam (Muslim "BAG") would solve our basic problem of the impending holocaust at the hands of our former slavemasters' children. Be that as it may, even in the Muslim QU'RAN (Koran) there is an alleged "MIRACLE" which "AL'LAH PERFORMED" while proving to Moses, the African Jew, that He is:

...THE ONE AND ONLY TRUE GOD ... (Al'lah).

But the fact of any "...ONLY TRUE GOD..." does not change one problem of BLACK people anywhere. The story continued with the following dialogue between Moses and Al'lah. God (or Al'lah) to Moses:

...PLACE YOUR HANDS IN YOUR BOSSOM AND THEN PULL
IT FORTH; AND LO, <u>IT HAD TURNED WHITE</u>....

The words underlined are my doing for emphasis on the point in question. THINK! Would it have been a "MIRACLE" if Moses' "HANDS" were already "WHITE" when he placed them ...IN HIS "BOSSOM..."? Certainly not. It had to have been any other color than "WHITE," even technicolor at least. But, in this modern era where African people in the United States of America are "RUNNING LIKE CRAZY" to join the religion of another of their former slavemasters' children, they forgot that Arab Muslims were the ones who first started "...SHIPPING AFRICANS (from Africa's East Coast) TO ARABIA..." and other parts of southwestern Asia, as chattels, ir-respective of how many AFRICAN SLAVES became "SULTANS" or other "HEAD OF STATE." And these Muslims, like their BLACK ISRAELITE brothers and sisters, await their own God - AL'LAH - to perform another "MIRACLE" as "JEHOVAH" (Al'lah's competitor) did for Moses, Jesus Christ, and even Mohamet ibn Abdullah. As a direct result of our constant waiting for some "God" or another to do what we must do for ourselves, the "MIRACLE" that "Al'lah" performed for Moses, if ever such happened, suddenly take on the same attributes as that which Jehovah performed for Noah (Noe) in turning "CHANAAN" and his alleged "NEGRO CHILDREN" to the co-color they now have - "COLOURED."* In all of these areas (palaeontological, anthropological, and ethnological) the "CAUCASIANISTS, SEMITICISTS", and "HAMITICISTS," prove themselves to be in unity. They have also done extremely well in suppressing the RACIST and RELIGIOUSLY BIGOTED aspects of the works of their 'sacred "God-INSPIRED" ancestors' writings on how GOD (Jehovah, Jesus Christ, Al'lah, and all others) praised the so-called "NEGROES" of the Biblical Era, before, and after. The major tragedy of all of this is that hundreds of thousands of African people all over the world remain ignorant of all of these aspects of their indigenous African ancestral history and heritage. Not only are they ignorant of these facts; they, too often, prattle what they have been told by WHITE RACISTS and RELIGIOUS BIGOTS (Christians as well as Jews, and others) their God has done to them in making the "CURSE" by Noah come true - "THEIR EN-SLAVEMENT TO THE CHILDREN OF SEM " ("Semites") because they "...GAZED AT..." grandfather Noah's (Noe, the father of Ham) NAKEDNESS...." One must wonder very seriously; how can a BLACK person who knows his or her self not exposed this type of SEMITIC RACISM and RELIGIOUS WHITEMAIL (bigotry)?

In an origin which modern theologians concede the "NEGROES" had (in the Indo-European, Aryan, Caucasian, Semitic, and Hamitic "GARDEN OF EDEN" around the Tigris and Euphrates valleys of southwestern Asia, not the Garden of Eden in central East Africa where the oldest known "HUMANOIDS" that dates back to miilions of years before the mythical birth of a SEMITIC " Adam and Eve), GOD had to be a WHITE CAUCASIAN with a "SEMITIC NOSE;" anything less than this professional "SEMITES" and "CAUCASIANS" could not accept. Yet, in a SEMITIC HEAVEN Caucasians, Indo-Europeans, Aryans, and Hamites, equally, could not feel at ease, or at home; thus, the "SEMITIC NOSE" became a "NORDIC NOSE." Why? Because the CAUCASIANS "pay the fiddler and call the tune. "Of course in both of the

---

*There is very little difference in the validity of the terms "NEGRO" and "COLOURED" or "COLORED;" both being the result of European and European-American RACISM against people of other "RACIAL ORIGINS."

46

HEAVENS mentioned, God - Jehovah, Jesus Christ, or Al'lah (depending upon one's institutional religious affiliation), could not have had a "...BROAD NOSE, THICK LIPS, WOOLLY HAIR, AND BURNT OF SKIN..." (Black) like the ancient Africans of Egypt and other Nile Valley High-Cultures from which these three GODS' religions took their roots. This ethnological, or racial, relationship between CAUCASIANS, SEMITES and HAMITES in a common beginning with "NEGROES" could not have happened, according to most of the modern ethnologists, paleontologists and anthropologists; even with the intersession of any of these three GODS who:

...MADE MAN IN HIS OWN IMAGE....

The GOD we are referring to, allegedly, "...MADE ALL OF THE PEOPLE OF THE MEDITERRANEAN WORLD..." like himself - "SEMITIC" if you are a Jew. "CAUCASIAN" if you are a White Christian, and "HAMITIC" if you are a dark-skinned European or brown-skinned Arabian from the Arabian Peninsula of southwestern Asia. You do not count in anyway whatsoever if you are just another BLACK-SKINNED any body. Thus, our "NEGRO-LESS" Caucasian and Semitic Egypt and Libya; also, our "NEGRO-LESS" Kush (Ethiopia) and Puanit or Punt (Somalia). Of course "modern EDUCATORS" who continuously perpetuate these illusions are blinded to the fact that the Nile Valleys (Blue and White) High-Cultures (civilizations) that reached their ZENITH at the southern shore of the Kimit (Mediterranean) Sea had their beginning around the area of the Bonyoro States (Buganda and Uganda), the areas of eastern Kongo (Congo), Tanganyika (Tanzania) and Kenya. The last three nations were located around the Great Lakes area of Central Alkebu-lan (Africa). This fact is best demonstrated on the "PREHISTORIC MAP" of Africa by Albert Churchward, M.D., shown on page 42 of this work. But, professional "SEMITICISTS" and "CAUCASIANISTS" seem to have conveniently forgotten that all of the ancient Egyptian historians, long before the birth of the first European historian - Herodotus, wrote that their own "...ANCESTORS (the so-called "Negroes") CAME FROM THE LANDS AT THE SOUTH OF THE MOUNTAIN OF THE MOON AT THE BEGINNING OF THE NILE.* This historical fact most certainly placed the origin of the ancient Egyptians and other North Africans of their era in "AFRICA SOUTH OF THE SAHARA." They have equally forgotten that to the immediate SOUTH of Egypt stood her sister nation, NUBIA (home of the "NUBIANS,

_____
* The Nile River was one of the GODS of the Egyptian religion; its name -"HAPI."

47

not "Negroes, Nilotes, Negroids, Hamites, or any other such "ITES, OTES, or "OIDS" created for Africa and Africans by so-called "WHITE LIBERAL AFRICANISTS"). Thus, they should remember that the NUBIANS were SOUTHERNERS who were embellished with the same type of PHYSICAL and COLOR characteristics the ancient Greek and Roman historians, philosophers, poets, etc. lavishly heaped upon the Egyptians in their description of them. All of the ancient European writers who wrote of the Africans of pre-Christian times said that the vast majority of them:

> ...HAVE THICK LIPS, BROAD NOSE, WOOLLY HAIR, AND THEY ARE BURNT OF SKIN....[41]*

Needless to say that the above quotation has been totally edited and re-edited (back and forth) by countless European and European-American **educators** who make it appear that the ancient Greeks and Romans could not have seen what they actually saw with regards to the North Africans "RACIAL" (physical) characteristics and "COLOR." In order to accomplish this end they have suppressed paintings, statues, pottery, and millions of other artifacts, that testify to the dominance of their so-called "NEGROES" in ancient North and East Africa. This evidence not only testifies to the dominance of "NEGROES" in North and East Africa alone, but also of those "NEGROES" who played a major role in the creation of the FIRST HIGH-CULTURES (civilizations) OF SOUTHERN EUROPE along the Kimit Sea. Their "NEGROES" were engaged in various periods of European prehistory and history. A few of them even became emperors of Rome. Of these, the most noted were Septimus Severus and his son - Caracalla "the tyrant".** This type of involvement by their "NEGROES" in the beginning of southern Europe's High-Culture (so-called "Western Civilization") predated Homer's ILLIAD and ODYSSEY, which he wrote in c. 600 B.C.E.[42]

AFRICA'S JUDAISM, CHRISTIANITY and ISLAM???

Whereas the synagogue protectors fear their "NEGRO ANCESTRY" which they inherited from Moses and their other ancestors who were enslaved by fellow

---

*This characterization is a direct quotation from Herodotus' HISTORIES, Book II. There are many such similar quotations from other Greek citizens and Romans throughout this, and others, work.
**See page 26 for bust of the African-Asian Emperor of Rome - Caracalla. Note his so-called "NEGROID" physical characteristics: "THICK LIPS, BROAD NOSE, CURLY HAIR." His father was an African from Khart Haddas (Carthage) and his mother an Asian from Assyria (Syria).

"NEGROES" of Egypt, North Africa; the church defenders, on the other hand
totally disclaim any ethnological affiliation (racial identity) with their
Mediterranean "SEMITIC" or "NEGROID" past. Yet, neither of these two groups has
been able to deny that both of these so-called "WESTERN RELIGIONS," Judaism and
Christianity, had their "SCRIPTURAL ORIGIN" in the landmass commonly called
"AFRICA" - originally "ALKEBU-LAN" by the Moors and Ethiopians.* But, the Jews**
cannot deny that before the birth of Moses, in Africa, there were no records of
any kind known to have been written by their so-called "Semitic ancestors."
The term "SEMITIC," as applied here, could be construed in a RELIGIOUS or
RACIAL sense; neither can change the facts. The Christians, on the other hand,
cannot deny that their religion's earliest "SCRIPTURES" came out of the same
place the Hebrews (Jews) got theirs, they being the offshoot of the Hebrews
that were converted into "followers of Jesus Christ" - who lived and died as a
fellow Hebrew or Jew. The Muslims, who adopted the basic tenets of their
religion from the Hebrew HOLY TORAH (Old Testament), the Christians HOLY BIBLE.
(New Testament) to form the HOLY QU'RAN (Koran)[43] cannot deny the role the
African - Hadzart Bilal ibn Rahbad (an Ethiopian from Kush, the place modern
Arabians called "ABYSSINIA") played in teaching their PROPHET - Mohamet ibn
Abdullah, and his writing of some of the most "SACRED SCRIPTURES" dealing with
"heavenly scenes."

Since "RACE," primarily defined through one's color of skin and facial
characteristics, has become the most important RELIGION in European and European-American society (Western Civilization), second only to MONEY, it should
be of no surprise to any African-American or African-Caribbean that those who
control said "SOCIETY" should have made their own "RACE superior to all others."
Here in the United States of American and its related Caribbean and Pacific
colonies, also in Europe and Britain, it is the members of the "GREAT WHITE
RACE," Semites and Hamites included, who declared themselves "...GOD'S CHOSEN
PEOPLE." However, we have become accustomed only to regard European and Euro-

---

*See Map of 1688 A.D., page 18, showing names Africa was called by the ancients
Before the Christian Era (B.C.E. or B.C.).
**This includes "Jewish" (Hebrew) people of every color and physical character-
istics - African, Asian, European, and European-American.

pean-American (WHITE) Jews, so-called "SEMITIC GROUP," as "GOD'S CHOSEN PEOPLE" because of the enslavement of many of us to the "King James Version" (TESTAMENT) of Judaeo-Christian mysticism - commonly called "THE CHRISTIAN HOLY BIBLE." This BIBLE, especially the BOOK OF EXODUS, is overloaded with anti-Egyptian (African) RACISM and RELIGIOUS BIGOTRY; and its usual pictorial illustrations maintain the image of a LILLY-WHITE HEAVEN to suit European-American SCRIPTURAL declarations, allegedly the "...HOLY WORDS OF GOD." The latter personality, "GOD," being either Jesus Christ or Jehovah, depends upon which religion one holds dear to his or her religious belief. This aspect of the entire BIG LIE of a "NEGRO-LESS" Judaeo-Christian and Islamic MYSTICISM brings back to memory an article in TIME MAGAZINE of July 5, 1971, page 59, under the caption: "JESUS WILL BE BLOND, JUDAS BLACK." This article dealt with the new rock opera - "JESUS CHRIST SUPERSTAR." Certainly you are correct in drawing the conclusion that you knew who was going to be Jesus Christ when there was to be an "INTEGRATED CAST." Of course a BLOND, BLUE-EYED, CAUCASIAN; the only thing missing being the necessary "SEMITIC" tinge. But this was already inherent in the fact that "SUPERSTAR" himself is alleged to have been a "SEMITE," the son of "JEWISH PARENTS" - Joseph and Mary;[44] both of them also PURE WHITE. At this point we must remember that daddy - "JOSEPH" - was only a guardian to "SUPER-STAR;" an "ANGEL" having brought him, instead of the usual "STORK." It certainly had to follow in a true RACIST form, according to the "AMERICAN DREAM," that "JUDAS" was IMPURELY BLACK - a typical soul brother from one of the Harlems of the United States of America. This type of selectivity is quite "AMERICAN" in character; it could not have been done much more efficiently in the "BIBLE BELT" - the so-called "...DEEP SOUTH."

As the story continued one of "SUPERSTAR'S" personal representatives on the planet EARTH (the "Western World" in particular), the Right Honourable "Evangelist" Billy Graham, is alleged to have protested the lack of the rock opera's dialogue's "...ATTESTING TO THE DIVINITY OF CHRIST..." rather than to "...THE QUESTION OF HIS BEING." Surely the Reverend Graham, being true to his European-American Judaeo-Christian form, did not object to '...THE USUAL CASTING OF AFRICAN PEOPLE AS DEVILS AND ANGELS...' whenever, and wherever, an

"INTEGRATED CAST" acts in any biblical scene; soul brother or sister never being "SUPERSTAR" or "JEHOVAH," not even an ANGEL or ADAM and EVE.

Somewhere along the line in this play a "SEMITIC" character other than by association had to appear; thus the so-called "JEWISH SOUNDING NAME" one is so accustomed to hear of in a DEMOCRACY - Yvonne "ELLIMAN." Correct again, Miss Elliman is not "JUDAS'" (the major BLACK figure of the play) mother. Naturally, she is MARY MAGDALENE - Superstar's "VIRGIN" mother. This too, is in keeping with the "HOLY FAMILY" and the "LAST SUPPER" Caucasian projections from the paintings of Michaelangelo, which were commissioned by Christendom's highest authority - its Pope in Rome. "Superstar," Jesus Christ, was able to maintain His BLOND WHITE SKIN, BLUE-EYES, and GOLDEN HAIR; all of this, in spite of the fact that he was born in a RED HOT Palestinian desert of BLACK and BROWN southwestern Asia (Asia-Minor, part of today's European-American Jewish state - ISRAEL).

## PASSING THE MYTH

I am compelled to bring to your attention another of the many ways in which the racist and religiously bigoted "SEMITIC" syndrome of a "NEGRO-LESS" North and East Africa passes on with the approval of innocent African people; some of whom are AFRICAN and BLACK Studies professors. In a book by Edmund David Cronon, published by the University of Wisconsin Press (Madison, Milwaukee, and London), 1968, commonly used in BLACK Studies Courses, there appears to be a kind of honest effort on the part of this European-American author to be IMPARTIAL in his treatment of the political life of one of the most noted and distinguished BLACK MEN the "Western World" has ever produced - MARCUS MOSIAH (Arellius) GARVEY, the late "Provisional President - General of Africa." The late Honourable Mr. Garvey (founder of the UNIVERSAL NEGRO IMPROVEMENT ASSOCIATION (U.N.I.A.), whose "BACK TO AFRICA" nationalist stance Dr. W.E.B. DuBois and A. Phillip Randolph (along with others of their political philosophy) fought "tooth-and-nail" to protect their own pet AMALGAMATION and INTEGRATION programs of the National Association for the Advancement of Coloured People (N.A.A.C.P.), was also the creator of the "TRI-COLOR FLAG OF

AFRICA"* which the so-called modern "WHITE NEW LEFT" worshippers of Dr. DuBois claimed is the "BLACK LIBERATION FLAG." This very short background on Garvey, which digressed from the main theme, is necessary if we are to understand the full impact of the following comments.

Cronon's book, widely accepted by Afro-American "New Left MILITANTS," obviously should be shared in the same manner by this writer. Maybe so, providing that I am willing to assume that the late Honourable Marcus Mosiah Garvey[45] was a "GOOD MAN FOR THE NEGRO PEOPLE," even though a bit "BOMBASTIC." Of course any self respecting African or African-American cannot tolerate for one solitary moment this type of WHITE RACIST characterization of one of Africa's greatest sons, who gave his life in the struggle to keep African people all over the world from the acts of slavery by Europeans and European-Americans; and from the pending hollocaust of genocide being prepared for African peoples by European-Americans for the very near future. However, the major tragedy of this book is not within the pages of its contents; it appears as you take it up and read the cover: "BLACK MOSES," the title of the book. "What is so offensive about this title" some BLACK STUDIES professors asked? The following is only a few of the answers:

a). It presupposes that "Moses," an African of Egypt, if in fact such a person ever existed other than in the mind of the writers of the Great Synagogue who wrote what is supposed to have been Moses' First through Fifth books of the Holy Torah, was some color other than "BLACK."

b). Mr. Garvey is not projected as a modern Pharaoh Rameses II, the African King of Egypt who chased Moses for breaking LAW AND ORDER when he committed murder (a violation of the so-called "TEN COMMAND-MENTS" he was supposed to have "received from Jehovah at Mount Sinai" some "forty (40) years" later; ten out of the one hundred and forty-seven (147) NEGATIVE CONFESSIONS of the Osirian Drama used throughout Nile Valley High-Cultures before the birth of Moses by more than three thousand and five hundred (3,500) years). If a BLACK man in the United States of America killed one of President Nixon's "WARRIORS," would he not be hunted-down for violating LAW AND ORDER? Garvey fought for LAW AND

---

*These colors were copied from the national flag of Alkebu-lan's (Africa's) ZENJ EMPIRE. This EMPIRE was located on Alkebu-lan's East Coast, along the Red Sea. Note that the "African" fossil-man, "ZINJANTHROPUS boisie," got its name from this source. The name Zenj was given to this area of Alkebu-lan by invaders from Persia (today's Iran).

ORDER; neither being possible for BLACKS in a "Western Civilization."

c). Toussaint L'Overtoure of the Island of Hayte (Haiti) led his African brothers and sisters in a death-struggle against European colonial slavery and genocide directed against them; and defeated Napoleon Boneparte's Caribbean naval fleet and freed his people from French imperialism. Why not name Garvey after him. This was no earlier than 1792 C.E., sixteen (16) short years after Haitians fought with General Lafayeete to free WHITE AMERICA from WHITE GREAT BRITAIN in 1776 C.E. (General George Washington of British-America vs. King George IIIrd of Great Britain).

d). Quacko and other Maroon leaders of Jamaica, an island of the Caribbean Sea where Mr. Garvey was born of similar family background, defeated British military forces and seized part of the island as "African free land;" all of this during the latter part of the 19th century C.E. Why not call Garvey the MODERN QUACKO?

Mr. Garvey could not be equated to any of the above people, nor to Denmark Vesey, Cato, or Nat Turner, because this would have given young BLACK-AMERICANS a sense of feeling that they should imitate him. For the same reason none of the above noted late African-Americans is being praised in the United States of America's churches and synagogues in the same manner as Jesus Christ or Moses. Yet all of them did no less, or tried to do no less, than Moses or Jesus Christ against SLAVERY, GENOCIDE, and RACISM, RELIGIOUS BIGOTRY not excluded, in their lifetime. There are many other reasons which are much more basic to the theme of this area of CAUCASIANISM and SEMITISM African-Americans are confronted with in these United States of America. The following is only a few:

a). In order for any African-American or African-Caribbean to be considered KOSHER he or she must have imitated someone of a WHITE Judaeo-Christian European-American (Anglo-Saxon Protestant Christian preferable) image.

b). No so-called "NEGRO" in the common thinking generally displayed by "CAUCASIANS" (Jewish or Christian), Greek-centric or not, is considered a KOSHER AMERICAN unless he, or she, professes some kind of Christian or Jewish affiliation, preferable BAPTIST PROTESTANTISM; Roman Catholicism as a poor second choice; Judaism with all kinds of apprehension; and Islam with the gravest of dismay - but better off than any so-called "HEATHEN RELIGION" from Africa.

The selection of this title, "BLACK MOSES," with respect to "the greatest hero of BLACK PEOPLE" (African people, not "NEGROES"), in a society where it

53

has been forever taught that Jews are "SEMITES," and of late even "WHITE
CAUCASIANS," it is an INSULT to have named the late Honorable Marcus Moziah
Garvey - "Provisional President-General of Africa," founder of the "BACK TO
AFRICA MOVEMENT"[46] of the early 20ᵗʰ century C.E., in honour of a WHITE CAU-
CASIAN and SEMITICALLY PROJECTED MOSES who was in violation of African LAW
AND ORDER. Marcus Moziah Garvey, a BLACK MAN, was prosecuted and persecuted
for allegedly VIOLATING WHITE AMERICA'S (Christian and Jewish) "LAW AND ORDER"
in the process of doing what was necessary for the cause of freedom for his
fellow-African people from European and European-American (WHITE-Christian,
Jewish, and others) institutions of slavery and genocide. All of this, I must
remind you, is only based upon the fact that the African, "MOSES," has been
projected by Cronon as something other than a "BLACK Man." Needless to say
that there is no evidence whatsoever in any BOOK or SCROLL of antiquity, around
the era of Moses' lifetime in Africa (c. 1318-1192 B.C.E., from Pharaoh Seti I
to beyond Pharaoh Rameses II - the XIXᵗʰ Dynasty according to the African High
Priest Manetho's chronological dating of Egypt's dynastic reigns), which
describes his facial characteristics or color of skin in any way different to
any other African (Egyptian) Herodotus and all of the other ancient writers
mentioned. As a matter of fact, the closest means of any "RACIAL" identification
there is of this man, MOSES, comes from the Haribu (Jewish) Holy Torah; a
quotation from the SECOND BOOK OF MOSES (otherwise called "EXODUS"), Chapter II,
Verses 15-22. In this explanation we find Moses' future wife saying to her
father - the High Priest of Media :

"...THAT EGYPTIAN HELPED ME..."

The young woman, whom he eventually married, could not distinguish Moses from
any other Egyptian (indigenous "Ethiopians" or "Negroes") she knew. She was
very positive of his physical identification, also geo-politically; but she
mentioned nothing that indicated he worshipped any other God than the God RA
which the general Egyptian population worshipped at that period in mankind's
history, She did not recognize him as a JEW or HARIBU. As a matter-of-fact,
Moses was not himself a member of the TRIBE OF JUDAH, thus he could not have
been a "JEW." According to the SECOND BOOK OF MOSES, which he was supposed to
have approved, if not written, he is presented as a LEVITE - a member of the

54

"...TRIBE OF LEVI." Stranger yet, both LEVI and JUDAH were direct descendants of NOAH, HAM, SEM, CHANAAN. Even JESUS CHRIST and MOHAMET ibn ABDULLAH were descendants of the same NOAH, who in turn was directly descended from "ADAM" and "EVE," according to the same "HOLY SCRIPTURE" which supposedly was totally "...WRITTEN BY GOD-INSPIRED HOLY MEN..." But not one of them, we are to assume, was a "NEGRO." A "NEGRO" could not possibly be "GOD-INSPIRED." WHY? Because a SEMITIC Jehovah (GOD), allegedly, "...TURNED NEGROES BLACK" when they were "...CURSED..." by a common "DRUNK" who got loaded on SNEAKY PETE ("grape wine" from Noah's own vineyard); all because one of them - "HAM ...STARED AT HIS FATHER'S ("Noah") NAKEDNESS...," but did not stare at his MOTHER'S "NAKEDNESS." Stranger yet. It is commonly held by most of the Caucasianists and Semiticists, many of whom are otherwise called "THEOLOGIANS" and "MEMBERS OF THE CLERGY," particularly those of the LATTER DAY SAINTS (Mormons) and Calvinist DUTCH REFORM movement, that the color "BLACK IS THE MARK OF THE CURSE GOD"...(of course the Christians' Jesus Christ or the Jews' Jehovah - the WHITE ones only)..."PLACED UPON THE CHILDREN OF CANAAN" (Negroes). In this regard; is it any wonder that so many young BLACKS (African-Americans) are rejecting all religions based upon a Judaeo-Christian and Islamic heritage? It should not be; for nowhere in history has there ever been any other people who has lived through the BLACK PEOPLE'S experiences of attacks of genocide and slavery and still continue worshipping their slavemasters' GOD. This statement includes every consideration for European and European-American (white) Jews, as African and African-American (Black) Jews also suffered equally with other BLACK people in slavery and genocide. BLACK JEWS also suffered from the sixth (6th) century C.E. WHITE JEWISH "scholars" RACIST propaganda about the Noah-Chanaan fairy tale they projected out of context in the Genesis myth. This continues, because African-Americans have not yet learned that no other people have continued worshipping another's God, especially their SLAVEMASTER'S God or Gods, and freed themselves from cultural and physical genocide. Why should Africans and African-Americans be the only exception to this historic reality? The proof that this will never happen in the case of BLACKS, so far as their former slavemasters' children are concerned, is most evident in the RACIST

GENTLEMEN'S AGREEMENT prevalent among most Europeans and European-Americans to
..."KEEP THE NIGGERS IN THEIR PLACE." When one adds the ETHNOCENTRICITY of the
"SEMITIC" syndrome to the so-called "LIBERAL JEWISH FRIENDS OF THE AMERICAN
NEGROES" and the "JEWISH-NEGRO COALITION FOR NON-VIOLENT ACTION" one hears so
much about of late from members of the National Association for the Advancement
of Coloured People (N.A.A.C.P.) and the National Urban League (N.U.L.), one
can better realize why"TOTAL FREEDOM"from European and European-American
(Christian, Jews, and others alike) OPPRESSION, SLAVERY and GENOCIDE, is im-
practical from an INTEGRATIONIST and NON-VIOLENT projection. Further proof in
this area is historical. Evidence of this nature has been best demonstrated in
the withdrawal of such "...LIBERAL WHITE FRIENDS OF THE NEGROES..." from the
Congress of Racial Equality (C.O.R.E.) when said ..."COLORED ORGANIZATION'S"...
African-American leadership decided to adopt a "BLACK NATIONALIST" stance,
instead of continuing the weary and wornout "INTEGRATION" and "AMALGAMATION"
myths established by the former "WHITE LIBERALS" (Jews and Christians) who
dominated C.O.R.E.'s Board of Directors. In otherwords; neither "WHITE" Jews
nor Christians, athiests and others included, can TRULY accept BLACK-AMERICANS
"independence of thought" towards their own freedom from slavery and genoicde,
even when they are in command of how it is to be gained; especially when such
a "dangerous thought" is directed towards the ECONOMIC INTERESTS of the so-
called "WHITE LIBERALS" and the immediate funds that pay what they call in
private "the H.N.C." - "HEAD NIGGERS IN-CHARGE," or their much more frightened
"FIELD NIGGERS." Thus, one can safely say that the current children of the most
recent"ex-slaves"in human history - the so-called "NEGROES" - cannot, should
not, and will not, expect any honest degree of help towards our freedom from
the inheritors of the wealth that was made on the backs and graves of our
ancestors enslavement. This, of course, does not exclude the so-called White
"NEW LEFT, OLD LEFT, NEW RIGHT, OLD RIGHT, MARXISTS, CAPITALISTS," and others;
all having had their chance along with their "CAUCASIAN" and "SEMITIC" Gods.
They had their chance from the first moment the BLACK MAN - the African people
- was placed, and forced to remain, in the dastard misery of the Slave trade in

56

c. 1503 C.E.*[47] to the present 1971 C.E. On the otherhand the JACK-IN-THE-BOX
type of "NEGRO" and "COLOURED" organizations leadership should be free to lead
their ULTRA MIDDLE-CLASS anti-BLACK (African) NATIONALIST membership, along
with their "WHITE LIBERAL FRIENDS OF THE NEGRO-WHITE COALITION," to the pro-
miseländ of "INTEGRATION" and "AMALGAMATION." What other purpose can the latter
serve? They seem only to be able to perform in the cause of "BONDS FOR ISRAEL,
GIFTS FOR IRELAND," and "PACKAGES FOR PAKISTAN," but never for a piece of 'RAG FOR
AFRICA' unless the "WHITE COALITION" is ready to go "HEATHEN" - as seen in the
case when the unholy alliance between WHITE PROTESTANT and ROMAN CATHOLIC
European-American style "Christian" joined White JEWISH "peace-loving" and "God-
fearing CHOSEN PEOPLE" to "SAVE THE IBO RACE FROM THE AFRICAN SAVAGES OF
NORTHERN AND WESTERN NIGERIA WHO ARE COMMITTING GENOCIDE AGAINST THEM." Of
course, it was obvious that the WHITE members of the same "COALITION" never
thought for one moment that "GENOCIDE" being committed in the southern half of
Africa by White CHRISTIANS and JEWS should be equally attacked other than by a
few senseless "BOYCOTTS" of lobsters from South Africa and the "WITHDRAWAL OF A
FEW DOLLARS" from one of Nelson Rockefeller's and other "WHITE LIBERALS'" number of banking institutions and international cartels. How effective can "NE-
GROES" move against those "WHITE LIBERALS" who provided them with new churches,
homes, and jobs; who even eat with them and play on the same golf course? The
answer to the latter is best demonstarted in the "GOOD NEGROES" frightening
quietness and resignation to the 'mass genocide' committed against African-
Americans and African-Puerto Ricans in Rockefeller's Attica State Prison on
September 13, 1971, at which time at least thirty one (31) helpless African
people** were brutally exterminated on the orders of "WHITE LIBERAL FRIENDS OF
THE NEGRO PEOPLE."

"NEGRO" DEDICATION TO OTHERS FREEDOM

The "SEMITIC" syndrome even forced "non-violent Negro Leaders" to sign all
kinds of "PETITION FOR MILITARY PLANES AND GUNS FOR ISRAEL," but not the first
PETITION for a single PEA-SHOOTER for the Africans (Black People As Themselves)

---

*The year Rt. Rev. Bishop Bartolome de LasCasas of the Roman Catholic Church
started the infamous slave trade to the Americas. See Note 47 for further details.
**The vast majority of Puerto Ricans are of African ancestry as the so-called

fighting against European and European-American dispensers of GENOCIDE in Angola, Mozambique, Southwest Africa and the so-called "Republic of South Africa." In the "Republic of South Africa," for example, JEWS,* CHRISTIANS, and other "GOD-FEARING" Whites, daily engage in the systematic extermination of the indigenous African people at a pace and severity far in excess of Adolph Hitler's 1938 C.E. attempted extermination of European Jewery. The "SEMITIC" syndrome goes even further than this. How often has "BLACK AND BEAUTIFUL" not listened to the radios of WHITE-AMERICA telling them that another "NEGRO LEADER" is "AGAINST Ki-SWAHILI BEING TAUGHT IN THE CITY OF NEW YORK'S PUBLIC SCHOOLS." Continuous echos of this nature have been voiced in the presence of so-called "SEMITIC PEOPLE" meeting in commemoration of their own cultural and religious "SEPARATISM" by many "NEGRO LEADERS" who dare not voice similar opinions against YIDDISH, HEBREW, GAELIC, ITALIAN, FRENCH, etc. presently being taught in the same schools. Today the ARCH-DUKE of ANTI whatever "Black Nationalists" desire as a possible alternative to bankrupt INTEGRATION and AMALGAMATION à-la National Association of the Advancement of Colored People and National Urban League is on another of his "GOOD COLOURED NEGRO LEADER" task. This "NON-VIOLENT" advocate of PETITIONS FOR GUNS FOR ISRAEL, one "brother" Rustin, is now DEAD-set on a course to prevent the adoption of courses in BLACK STUDIES dealing with "BLACK DIALECT" and "BLACK DIALOGUE." But, is it strange, or rather comical, that the good "brother" seems to be totally mute when it comes to objecting to YIDDISH DIALECT, a broken-down development of folkloric German and other European languages and dialects, English included, being taught in the same schools, or in colleges where White Nationalist Jewish students study. Maybe we will, or should, hear from the ARCH-DUKE when he finds out that all kinds of professors are already studying the so-called "DIALECT OF THE GULLAHS"[48] of the Carolina Islands.

CONFRONTATION

    Blacks are CONFRONTED with a very serious issue in any exposure of the pro-

---

"NEGROES" in America; both from the Africans of the West Coast of Africa, and African MOORS from the North.
*See THE NEW YORK POST, Monday, November 4, 1968, page 36, article entitled: "RABBI RAPS JEWS ON APARTHIED." For the general attitude towards non-White Jews in Israel today se the NEW YORK DAILY NEWS article of Thursday, July 29, 1971, page 16, entitled: "GOLDA SEEKS A HALT TO STRIFE IN ISRAEL," by Sigismund Goren (Special Correspondent of THE NEWS).

fessional SEMITE and the "SEMITIC" syndrome dealing with the exclusion of the so-called "NEGROES" from the prehistory and history of North and East Africa. The seriousness bypasses the fact that there is an abundance of substantiated data to prove the contrary; but in the fact that BLACKS feel that they should not, or cannot, attack the so-called "WHITE LIBERAL AFRICANOISTS" who masquerade under the protection of being "SEMITIC PEOPLE." WHY? Because BLACKS have also used the protection smoke-screen of hollering "ANTI-NEGROISM" when our so-called "LIBERAL WHITE FRIENDS" from left and right wanted us to do so to benefit their own interest economically and"racially." Since BLACKS have been doing this type of SCAPEGOAT action against the so-called "WHITE ANGLO-SAXON CHRISTIAN" along with our "WHITE SEMITIC" coalition partners, and we must depend largely, in some cases totally, upon the "COALITION'S" capital to pay our salaries and mortgages, etc., BLACKS cannot equally protest against "WHITE JEWISH ANTI-BLACKISM" or "ANTI-NEGROISM" with the same fervor employed against their "ANGLO-SAXON" fall-guys. This, of course, relates only to "BLACK NEGROES" and "COLOURED FOLK."

THE SEMITIC RACE MYTH

The cry of "ANTI-SEMITISM" shall never shut-up one BLACK person who will stick to documentary evidence for whatever is charged. The cry of "ANTI-SEMITISM" will not deter any member of the BLACK SEPARATIST movement, since they do not depend upon handouts from "SEMITIC" or "CAUCASIAN" sources. But the concept of a "JEWISH RACE," dispelled by many Jewish writers all through the centuries, has raised its ugly head once more. Unfortunately, it was not put to rest by M. Fishberg's most noted work: THE JEW, London, 1911; also G. A. Massey's, BOOK OF THE BEGINNINGS, London, 1881; and Nesfield's, BRIEF VIEW of the CASTE SYSTEM. This was to be expected when the State of Israel became a reality; as millions of EHITE JEWS failed to remember that their fellow BLACK JEWS are as much the descendants of the "BIBLE PEOPLE" (Chosen People) as they are, maybe moreso, especially the "FALASHAS" (Beta Israelis) of Ethiopia, "YEMENITES" of Yemen, and "COCHIMS" of India. The last three groups of Hebrews,[49] not "Jews," preservation of ancient Hebrew traditional culture and religion are unmatched by European and European-American Hasidic,

59

Sfardic, and Ashkanazic, European and European-American Jewish traditions.
Thus, the claim of a "JEWISH RACE" must be just as forcefully denounced by
BLACKS who are of Hebrew background; that is regardless of whether we are
active participants in the BLACK ISRAELITE NATION, or backsliders. Anything
short of this by BLACK ISRAELITES is Hitleric in kind; for this cancer has
even reached the point where actively participating BLACK ISRAELITES have to
prove their "Jewishness" to WHITE JEWS in order to have their approval and
GOOD KOSHER JEW stamp or lable. Yet, we must remember that a White or Black
JEW from the United States of America or Europe does not automatically become
a non-RACIST or non-RELIGIOUS BIGOT by virtue of fact that he or she has
migrated to what some still call "THE PROMISE LAND" - Israel. Today, for most
BLACK and BROWN JEWS (Israelites), WHITE RACISM in Israel still marrs their
"PROMISE," and prevents them from realizing a common "LAND" for ALL JEWS  -
regardless of "COLOR" or "RACE."

AFRICANS GLORY

        The Africans of the Western area of Africa, those South of the Sahara,
as well as those on the East, are not short of the glorious praises both
"CAUCASIANS" and "SEMITES" showered on them in times gone by; that is before
professional "SEMITICISTS" and "CAUCASIANISTS" found it intolerable to have
descended from the same common ancestor as their "NEGROES." In this light we
read the following from the CHRONICLES of a sixteenth (16th) century C.E.
Florentine merchant-traveler by the name of Francesco Carletti, a report of
his voyages made between the years 1591-1606 C.E.; the English title: MY
VOYAGE AROUND THE WORLD - the Italian: "Ragionamenti del mio viaggio intorno
al mondo." Carletti wrote:

        But the island of Sao Tiago, where we landed, lies
        sixteen degrees above the equinoctial line northwards,
        approximately fifteen hundred miles off Spain and three
        hundred miles from the land of Cape Verde on the con-
        tinent of Africa. On the island there is a little city
        called Nome de Deus, which has a moderately sized harbour
        facing toward the south. It has its bishops and inhab-
        itants of which number approximately fifty houses of
        married Portuguese men, many with white women from
        Portugal, some with black women of Africa, and others
        with mulatto women born on the island of white men
        and Moorish (or black, as we should say) women.

At this point, I could have stopped quoting from the work of this traveler of the 16ᵗʰ and 17ᵗʰ century Mediterranean "world," who obviously had no "CAUCASIAN" or "SEMITIC" skeletons to hide. But, I intend to elaborate on the point that the MOORS were called "BLACK," as were all other Africans of this area and period in "World History;" and nothing modern "SEMITICISTS" or "CAUCASIANISTS" can do will change this fact. The same holds true for **other** North Africans of this period, before, and after. The traveler continued:

> ...Their Portuguese men love these black women more than their own Portuguese women, believing in it as a proven fact that to have intercourse with them is much less injurious and much greater in pleasure, they being said to have fresher and healthier natures.

My reason for this apparent digression from the main theme should have become quite obvious before the traveler got to the point where he cited the Portuguese men's preference for the MOORISH (Black or "Negro") women; the same type that migrated from parts south of Egypt and aided in the building of its High-Cultures from prehistoric to historic times. Also, to remind you that along with the Portuguese Christians were the DeSolas', Cintrons', DaSilvas', Leones', and others - all of these olden names of the Jews who lived among the Portuguese in Portugal and migrated with them to their colonies all over the world. Such "SEMITES" also lived amongst the Moors in Spain, and under Moorish High-Culture, from 711 to 1485 C.E. During this period when the Moors ruled Spain White Christian and Jewish women had children for said Moors - ("NEGROES"), some as wives, and others as concubines.

ACTION AND POINT OF ATTACK

The best place in which to commence a reversal of the "SEMITIC" syndrome, on behalf of the BLACK MAN'S North and East African heritage and cultural history, is in the area of "AFRICAN STUDIES" and "BLACK STUDIES" where there is no African heritage base. The first change must be the use of an appropriately traditional name for African people. Thus, no "AFRO-AMERICAN;" there being no "O", whatsoever, in the word "AFRICA." Just as there is no Irish-American Studies without the teaching of Irish history and the culture of Ireland at its base, Jewish-American Studies without the teaching of Palestinian or Israeli culture, religion, and political heritage to meet WHITE Jewish values at its base; equally, it is also impossible to have Africa-less BLACK STUDIES courses. Can you imagine WHITE-American Jewish students accepting a Black (Israelite or not) - dominated "JEWISH STUDIES DEPARTMENT" in any of the institutions of learning (high or low) supported by them, their parents, or their rabbis? It will never happen. In this regard, you should not expect to see one in which "ZIONISM" is not stressed beyond the so-called "AMERICAN DREAM" (Judaeo-Christian Capitalism). Why, then, expect African-Americans to accept a PAN-AFRICAN-LESS "BLACK STUDIES DEPARTMENT" headed by WHITES (Jews, Christians, or others), where Africa is not projected as the "MAJOR PREMISE OF BLACK PEOPLE'S REDEMPTION" - a kind of "BLACK ZIONISM" if you please? Why should this view, when fostered by African-Americans, be any-the-less acceptable within the "American Dream" than Zionism? Because many of the same "SEMITICISTS" write and interpret both "JEWISH" and "NEGRO" history, and determine the destiny of each; BLACKS, for the most part, being unaware of this, "Negroes" condoning it.

BOOKS AND THE BLACKS

Why should books that determine BLACK AUTHORITATIVE SOURCES in "BLACK STUDIES" and "AFRICAN STUDIES" departments, for the most part, be written by WHITE professors (Jewish, Christian, or others) from their own WHITE MASTER-BLACK SLAVE perspective? Can anyone justify why the interpretations of what people of African origin must study should be that which the descendants of their ancestors slavemasters believe is MORAL or IMMORAL, TRUTH, or LIE? It is impossible (at least it should be) to expect that the interpretations of African history by Africa oriented professors of African origin will have the same conclusions as those who profess their own White "CAUCASIAN" and "SEMITIC" superior RACIAL origin that include all of North Africa, and much of the eastern part of the same continent, being solely of their origin. The mere profestation of "ACADEMIC SCHOLARSHIP" on the part of "WHITE LIBERALS" is without foundation in this arena of morality and political consideration, much less RACIALLY. It is like believing that Israeli Prime Minister Golda Meir could be solely "ACADEMIC" in her "SCHOLARSHIP" in teaching ARAB HISTORY to the children of the late President Abdul Gamal Nasser of Egypt. Would this be ARAB HISTORY AND CULTURE from an ARAB POINT OF VIEW, or the reverse? Not at all.

62

Neither is it possible for the professional "SEMITICISTS" or "CAUCASIANISTS" to write books complimentary to the African peoples' religions, cultures, political institutions and other life-styles, in competition of their own, irrespective of how many years they spend among any group of African people; RACISM and RELIGIOUS BIGOTRY being too much of the very embryo of European and European-American ("Western") society. There are at present too many books in "AFRICAN" and "BLACK" studies courses written by so-called "WHITE LIBERAL AFRICANISTS." For there is no such animal as a "WHITE LIBERAL AFRICANIST" who can see Africa and her sons' and daughters' history and cultural heritage in terms of an African historian who is dedicated to bringing to light the White RACIST plagiarization and suppression of Africa's past and/or present glory. But, what common statement will truly set this point in its proper perspective? Maybe none will cover all of the possible ills connected thereto; but the following is the closest I can think of at this juncture. That is:

THE HISTORY OF A PEOPLE IS THE INTERPRETED FACTS,
AS SEEN FROM THEIR OWN PREJUDICE EYES, WITH RELATION-
SHIP TO THEIR EXPERIENCES WITH THEMSELVES AND OTHERS.

For example: George Washington is a hero for all "PATRIOTIC WHITE AMERICANS" and "NEGROES." Why should African-Americans (BLACKS) feel the same about a man who was a master of cultural and physical genocide to their ancestors when he was their slavemaster? He was a WHITE man who saw AFRICAN PEOPLE being less than HUMAN, and treated them as such, at a period in history when he and all of the other WHITES who signed the "DECLARATION OF INDEPENDENCE" were fighting to be recognized as "FREE MEN." For some people, both BLACK and WHITE, even Adolph Eichman was great. Was he for the White Jews? African-American, as African history can only be truly interpreted to suit the BLACK MAN'S needs by BLACK oriented HISTORIANS. There can be no exception to this rule. Why? Because "WHITE STUDIES" books and their interpretations have been established by WHITE PROFESSORS in WHITE INSTITUTIONS, for WHITE STUDENTS and anyone-else who may stop by for their EUROPEANIZATION.[52] And no man in this culture can help injecting his own RACIST philosophy into another's history and heritage within this RACE-centric Judaeo-Christian-capitalist asylum. WHY SHOULD THE BLACK MAN NOT LEARN FROM HIS OWN PROFESSORS ABOUT HIS OWN GOD, or GODS, AND ABOUT HIS OWN "CHOSEN PEOPLE" - His mother, His father, and His family?

THE CALL

No longer shall BLACK PEOPLE remove themselves from the pages of North and East Africa's history on the directives of the children of their ancestors slavemasters. No longer shall BLACK PEOPLE stay quiet and listen to White or Black professors prattle their contempteous history of a "BLACK-LESS" Moorish history of Spain. No longer shall BLACK PEOPLE sit back and look at European-ized versions of HANNIBAL BARCA, GENERAL TARIKH, SEPTIMUS SEVERUS, ST. AUGUSTINE, ST. CYPRIAN, TERTULLIAN, AESOP, PIETRO OLONZO NIÑO, PIANKHI, HATSHEPSUT, MAKEDA or QUEEN OF SHEBA, AHA or MENES, IMHOTEP or AESCALAPIUS, and countless other BLACKS, and keep their mouth sealed while their anguish ravages their heart and soul. No longer shall BLACK PEOPLE bear witness to ZINJANTHROPUS BOISIE, AIMBABWE (Rhodesia) MAN, BOSKOP MAN, BROKEN HILL MAN, and other African prehistoric fossil-men being presented as "CAUCASIANS" and not protest in the strongest of avenues available to us; even to the point of violent action.

NORTH, SOUTH, EAST, WEST, AND CENTRAL ALKEBU-LAN (Africa) is the home and original "GARDEN OF EDEN" of the BLACK PEOPLES OF THE WORLD; whether they be in Australia, the Fiji Islands, the "Western Hemisphere," India, the Americas, Europe, or even Antarctica. If the WHITE Jews can claim a piece of land stolen by their ancestors from the JEBUSITES, AMALAKITES, PEZARITES, MOABITES, and other SITES; the AFRICAN PEOPLES of the "Western World" must equally have the right to claim their homeland, "MOTHER AFRICA," which they have not stolen from anyone in this entire world.

North and East Africa, so far as its ancient history and High-Cultures are concerned, is what it has always been from the time the first BLACK MAN - "THE FIRST MAN" - moved from the African Great Lakes region and migrated to the North by way of the NILE RIVER VALLEY and spread all over North Africa; this being no less than he did in his southern and western journeys to Monomotapa and Ghana. The map on the following page by your author presents a hypothetical view of the ORIGINAL MAN and his FAMILY'S movements.

North and East Africa still remain "...THE LAND OF THE SUN-BURNT PEOPLES..."

A L K E B U - L A N of the God RA

(Land of the Sun People of the Nile Valley God RA).

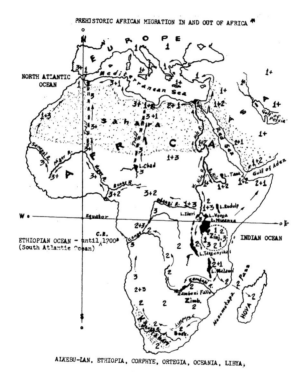

PREHISTORIC AFRICAN MIGRATION IN AND OUT OF AFRICA

ALKEBU-LAN, ETHIOPIA, CORPHYE, ORTEGIA, OCEANIA, LIBYA,

Akhenaten in the Royal Garden
with his wife, Nefertiti, and
one of his children. Note African physical characteristics.

Baron Viviant Denon's
drawing of the Great
Sphinx of Gizeh - the
face of Pharaoh Menke-
rere (Chephren) and
lion body. Note Afri-
can characteristics.

Black granite head of King Taharqa.

NOTES FOR CHAPTER I

1. Formerly an admiral in the navy of Spain during the reign of the Africans that captured Spain under their leader and general - Tarikh - for whom the Rock of Gibraltar - Gibral Tarikh or Tarikh Rock - got its name; the Moors having lost their power in approximately 1485 C.E. when the last of them were toppled in Granada.

2. The ancient Greeks and Romans misnamed it "Africa."

3. "NEGROES;" from the degrading term given people of Alkebu-lan by the Portuguese around the 16ᵗʰ or 17ᵗʰ century C.E. See BLACK MAN OF THE NILE, p. 267, showing area of Africa the Portuguese named "NEGROLAND."

4. Many "Western" historians differ on this data; they claim a period from about 800 to 600 B.C.E., depending on each writer.

5. THE CONQUEST OF CIVILIZATION, Harper & Row Publishers, N.Y., 1954 (fully revised by E. W. Ware, Ph.D.; first published by James H. Breasted in 1926 and 1938 - the author).

6. Basil Davidson, THE AFRICAN PAST: Chronicles From Antiquity To Modern Times, Little, Brown and Company, (Boston, Toronto), 1964.

7. Oxford University Press, 1970, Second Edition.

8. Two Romans, Paulnius Flaccus and Julius Maternus (c. 25-50 B.C.E.), wrote about these African Kingdoms.

9. Use of the CHRONOLOGICAL CHART on pages 96 through 103 (number at the bottom of the pages) of BLACK MAN OF THE NILE, Alkebu-lan Books Associates, New York, 1970, should be of major assistance. There are many other chronologies of this nature you may use. See also pages 306-313 of AFRICA: MOTHER OF "WESTERN CIVILIZATION," New York, 1971.

10. Modern geographic boundaries between these nations cannot apply. They were established by European and European-American imperialist slavetraders and colonialists at the 1884-85 C.E. BERLIN CONFERENCE ON THE REGULATION OF WEST AFRICAN TRADES AND TARIFFS that resulted in the Berlin "ACT." Not one African or Asian was allowed to have anything to say or do with the "ACT." It was a RACIST "CONFERENCE," and resulted in a RACIST "ACT." This should bring you to the point of understanding that the United States of America was totally involved in the PARTITION and COLONIZATION of Africa, sending her own envoy - Edwin H. Terrell, Envoy Extraordinary and Minister Plenipotentiary, to negotiate her interest in carving-up Africa and the extermination of its people. See PROTOCOL of Berlin Act, Trade and Civilization, Rivers Congo, Niger, etc., Slave Trade by Sea and Land, Feb. 2, 1892.

11. Named in honor of the African general, TARIKH, that defeated the Europeans of the Iberian Peninsula (Iberia) in 711 C.E. and took Mons Calpe - which his officers renamed "GIBRAL TARIKH" or Rock of Tarikh. These Africans were called Moors because they invaded Europe from Morocco; but they originally came from further south along the African west coast - Maueritania. Modern Mauritania occupies much of that ancient empire's landmass. Ancient Cerene is actually modern HERNE ISLAND at the entrance to the Senegal River in West Africa. See Stanley Lane-Poole, THE MOORS IN SPAIN, G. Putman's Sons, N.Y. & London, 1886, for further details on this area of Africa's history with respect to her sons in Iberia.

12. De incredibilibus 31 (32) in: MYTHOGRAPHI GRAECI, III, 2 (Leipzig, 1902, an edition by N. Festa).

13. PERIPLUS OF SCYLAX, GGM, I. 94.

14. PERIPLUS OF SCYLAX, GGM. I. 94.

15. Frg. 16, H. Diels, Die Fragmente der Vorsokratiker (Berlin 1961).

16. Ethiopie (Itiopi or Ethiopia, Kush) was a country; also the name of the entire continent the Greeks and Romans renamed "AFRICA" after their very small settlement they had on the seacoast of Lebus (Libya) before they were allowed to enter Kimit (Egypt) in mass before the arrival of the Hyksos invaders from Asia around c. 1675 B.C.E.

17. Later on this capital was moved to NAPATA, just as it was when the Kushites and Nubians ruled Egypt.

18. M. N. Tod, A SELECTION OF GREEK HISTORICAL INSCRIPTIONS, Oxford, 1946, Vol. I, no. 4.

19. Herodotus, HISTORIES, II., 152, 154. The Greeks also referred to a little PROVINCE they settled somewhere between Lebus (Libya) and Numidia as "AFRICA." See note 16 above for further details.

20. IMAGINES, I, 29; IMAGINES, I, 7.

21. The best examples of these Africans today are the so-called "HOTTENTOTS" and "BUSHMEN;" to some extent the so-called "PYGMIES." The correct name for the first two is KHOISAN PEOPLES; the latter is TWA.

22. Crown Publishers, Inc., New York, 1967 (as translated by A. E. Keep).

23. Do not forget their physical description and color detailed by the ancient Europeans before, and after, Homer to Herodotus -c. 600-c. 450 B.C.E.

24. Formerly Alexander's greatest general and his Governor of Egypt, SOTER, who declared himself - "PHARAOH PTOLEMY I RULER OF ALL EGYPT" - on the death of Alexander in c. 327 B.C.E. He became the original PATRIARCH of the Ptolemy line I (himself) to XV, which included the infamous Cleopatra VIII[th] who murdered her brother and uncle for the power of the throne, and made love to Caesar and Anthony to maintain said throne. The Ptolmey's MATRIARCH was the BLACK Egyptian ("Negro") Queen, Soter forced to become his wife upon assuming the Egyptian throne.

25. HAM, JAPHETH and SEM (Shem) had the same parents (mother and father); yet SEM'S and JAPHETH'S children and their offsprings became "SEMITES" in Europe and European-America with WHITE SKIN; whereas those of HAM'S son, CANAAN (Chanaan), became "NEGROES" in Africa and all other parts of the world, with BLACK SKIN. God, that is the Caucasian and Semitic, also Hamitic God, certainly "...ACTS IN MYSTERIOUS WAYS, HIS WONDERS NEVER CEASE." He even did the same when He changed Emperor Septimus Severus's son, CARACALLA (Shown on page **26** of this work), who was born of said African (BLACK or "NEGRO") father and an ASIAN - Syrian (BROWN) mother, a Nordic CAUCASIAN: yet we note the so-called "NEGRO" curled hair and heavy facial characteristics (thick lips, broad nose, mentioned by Herodotus and others) shown on the bust of Caracalla. He could certainly pass for any LIGHT-SKINNED "Negro" in the Harlems of the world, America in particular.

26. See page 266 (bottom numbers) of Yosef ben-Jochannan, BLACK MAN OF THE NILE, Alkebu-lan Books Associates, New York, 1970, for other names ALKEBU-LAN was called by the ancients. The author of this book is the writer of this work.

27. 18 A.H. was eighteen (18) years following the HEGIRA - the year Mohamet ibn Abdullah had to flee Mecca and seek refuge at the Oasis of Yathrib outside the city of Medina; his protectors being the Ethiopian army sent to his aid by Africans from whom his grandparents originated - in Ethiopia. See Yosef ben-Jochannan, AFRICAN ORIGIN OF THE MAJOR "WESTERN RELIGIONS," Alkebu-lan Books Associates, New York, 1970, Chapter IV; E. C. Hodgkin, THE ARABS,

Oxford University Press, Great Britain, 1966; P. K. Hitti, THE ARABS: A
SHORT HISTORY, St. Martins Press, New York, 1968; P. K. Hitti, MAKERS OF
ARAB HISTORY, St. Martins Press, New York, 1968; W. Montgomery Watt, WHAT
IS ISLAM?, Frederick Praeger, New York, 1968.

28. LasCasas imported more than 4000 Moors from Spain to the Island of
Hispaniola. This act initiated the Slave Trade of Africans to the "New
World." See Eric Williams DOCUMENTS OF WEST INDIAN HISTORY, 1492-1655,
PMN Publishing Co., Ltd., Trinidad, W.I., 1963, 4 vols; Brian Edwards,
HISTORY OF THE WEST INDIES, 1880; and Elizabeth Donnon, DOCUMENTS ILLUS-
TRATIVE of the HISTORY of THE SLAVE TRADE TO AMERICA, New York, 1935, 4
vols.; Eric Williams, FROM COLUMBUS TO CASTRO. THE HISTORY OF THE CARIB-
BEAN 1492-1969, Pub., by Andre Deutsch Ltd., London, 1970.

29. J. H. Lewis' book was listed because of its modern explanation with respect
to the topic. It is not an ancient work, and should not be treated as such.

30. The name the Romans and Greeks called Alkebu-lan.

31. The Nile River begins in today's Republic of Uganda and ends at the
Mediterranean Sea; more than 4,100 statute miles from south to north.

32. Kimit is the original name the indigenous Ethiopians called Egypt. They
also called it Sais, the name the earliest Greeks also called it. Egypt
is a name that had its origin in ancient Hebrew religious mythology -
especially as recited in the Holy Torah's Book of Genesis - the "FIRST
BOOK OF MOSES" - with respect to the tale about "Noah and the Flood."

33. Harvard University Press, Cambridge, Mass., 1970. In this work are artifacts
showing so-called "Negro" and "Negroid" features in every facet of Roman
and Greek society. Ethiopians (BLACKS or AFRICANS) appear as royalty in
these artifacts; equally as generals, statesmen and Gods; on legal currency
of many different materials they also appeared.

34. Millions upon millions of East, Central, North, West and South Africans
have pointed nose and thin lips. These characteristics were, and are,
common to Africans as they are to many other cultural groupings in Asia,
Europe and European-America. There were equally, thousands of ancient
Egyptians with pointed nose and thin lips before the arrival of the so-
called "SEMITIC PEOPLE" from Asia - the Hyksos. This fact is apparent in
almost every book published on Egypt since the first half of the 19th
century C.E.; for at this period artifacts of Egyptians with "Negroid"
features began to have objectionable meaning to those WHITES in control of
their stolen treasure - Egypt and everything in it.

35. BLUE in Ethiopia, WHITE in Uganda and Nubia (Sudan), BLUE and WHITE combined
in Nubia and Kimit (Sais, Mizrain or Egypt). 4100 statute miles from
Uganda (at Mwanza Nyanza - colonialist "Lake Victoria") to the Kimit
(Mediterranean) Sea. These High-Cultures shared a common heritage and
origin from the GREAT ALKES regions: Egypt, Nubia, Merowe, Ethiopia,
Zimbabwe, Dhlo-Dhlo, Ghana, Mali, Songhai, Khart Haddas, Numidia, Lebus,
and others. Central East Africa, around the OLDUVAI GORGE has proven to
be the original home of every one of these High-Cultures; and lately of
mankind in general (See Sonia Cole, A PREHISTORY OF EAST AFRICA, New York,
1963; L. S. B. Leakey, THE STONE AGE RACE OF KENYA, 1931; THE STONE AGE
CULTURES OF KENYA COLONY, 1935; ANTIQUITY, 1951, ibid.; W. E. Clark Le
Gross and L. S. B. Leakey, THE MIOCENE HOMINOIDEA OF EAST AFRICA, British
Museum of Natural History, London, 1951; H. L. Wells, "The Fossil Human
Skull from Singa" (in: PLEISTOCENE FAUNA OF TWO BLUE NILE SITES), British
Museum of Natural History, London, 1951.

36. Dictionnaire de la Civilisation Egyptienne, Paris 1959, (translated from
the French by Alix MacFarlane), Tudor Publishing Company, New York.

37. Today's so-called "Republic of South Africa" where the indigenous Africans are on concentration camps (otherwise called "Reservations"), is in many respects not unlike the United States of America where indigenous "Americans" (misnomered "Indians") are also penned in.

38. The United States of America engaged (to the hilt) in the PARTITION OF AFRICA through the activities of the American Colonization Society (White dominated), which it supported in granting two naval ships used to murder Africans of Liberia, West Africa. It also took part in said destruction of African High-Cultures at the BERLIN and BRUSSELS Conferences of 1884-1896 C.E. See Sir Edward Hertslett, THE MAP OF AFRICA BY TREATY, Her Majesty's Stationary Office, London, 1895, Vol. II; J. Scott-Keltie, THE PARTITION OF AFRICA, London, 1896.

39. C. P. Groves, THE PLANTING OF CHRISTIANITY IN AFRICA, Butterworth Press, London, 1948.

40. See J. Scott-Keltie, PARTITION OF AFRICA, London, 1896; Sir Edward Hertslett, THE MAP OF AFRICA BY TREATY, 3 vols, London; Y. ben-Jochannan, THE RAPE OF AFRICA AND THE CRISIS IN ANGOLA, Ghana, 1966 (pamphlet).

41. To distinguish between Egyptians and Nubians during the Dynastic Periods is an impossible task for any 17th, 18th, 19th or 20th century C.E. researcher who is not suffering from Negrophobia, Caucasianism or Semiticism. Either of these syndromes will make one find many races between the Egyptian and Nubian people of Alkebu-lan (Africa): Which the ancients were not aware existed. These High-Cultures shared common Gods, economies, science and technology, and even Law and Order as each group ruled the other. (See G. Jackson, INTRODUCTION TO AFRICAN CIVILIZATIONS, University Books, New York, 1970; G. C. M. James, STOLEN LEGACY, Philosophical Library, New York, 1954; Y. ben-Jochannan, AFRICA: MOTHER OF "WESTERN CIVILIZATION," New York, 1971; Sir J. Frazier, THE GOLDEN BOUGH, London, Macmillan and Co. Ltd., 13 vols.; G. Maspero, HISTORY OF EGYPT (transl. to English from the original French), Wm. Cloves and Sons, Ltd., London, 1886, 8 vols.; and Sir E. A. Wallis Budge, BOOK OF THE DEAD, London, 1884; and PAPYRUS OF ANI, London, 1884; Wm. Palmer, EGYPTIAN CHRONICLES, Longman, Green, Longman, and Roberts, London, 1861, 2 vols.; Sir E. A. Wallis Budge, A HISTORY OF EGYPT, Routledge & Kegan Paul Ltd., London, 1900, 4 vols.

42. In this area the best book for artifacts showing the influence of Ethiopians (the so-called "Negroes,") in ancient Rome and Greece see F. W. Snowden, BLACKS IN ANTIQUITY, etc., Harvard University Press, Cambridge, 1970.

43. See Chapter IV, AFRICAN ORIGINS OF THE MAJOR "WESTERN RELIGIONS," by Yosef ben-Jochannan, Alkebu-lan Books Associates, New York, 1970, for an entire outline on many of the contributions by Bilal to Islam; and his assistance to Mohamet in the creation of that which is today the MUSLIM RELIGION or the Islamic Nation. For added data See also J. A. Rogers, WORLD'S GREAT MEN OF COLOR, New York, 1947. Vol. 1; P. K. Hitti, HISTORY OF THE ARABS; Al-Jahiz, KITAB al-SUDAN WAL'BIDAN (English title: "The Superiority in the Glory of the Black Race over the White"); H. G. Wells, A SHORT HISTORY OF THE WORLD; P. K. Hitti, THE MAKING OF ARAB HISTORY; Bisland, LIFE AND LETTERS OF LAFCADIO HEARN.

44. In the LOST BOOKS OF THE BIBLE (The Book of Mary) it is shown that Mary - "Superstar's" mother - had a son named "James" when she was only thirteen (13), Superstar when she was twenty-eight (28), yet she remained a physical virgin to this very day. There is nothing "LOST" about the "Books" taken out of the Holy Bible at the Nicene Conference of Bishops in c. 322 C.E. ordered by Emperor Constantine "the great." They have been suppressed, because those who operate religious institutions as they do giant business enterprises for enormous profits are afraid of what would happen to said cartels should their parishioners find out the controversial tales hidden in the so-called "LOST BOOKS." You may purchase these missing books in one

work - LOST BOOKS OF THE BIBLE and the FORGOTTEN BOOKS OF EDEN, The World Publishing Co., Cleveland, Ohio, 1926.

45. The late Marcus Moziah (Arellius) Garvey organized the greatest "Back To Africa movement" throughout the world, even exceding the Pan-African Congress (all six) conferences by DuBois and Padmore. Garvey's movement was all B ack; the other "INTEGRATED." See PHILOSOPHY AND OPINIONS OF MARCUS GARVEY, Frank Cass & Co. Ltd., 1967, (First Edition, Part I, 1923, Part II, 1925; Second Edition, Part I, 1967, Part II, 1967); Edmund Cronon, BLACK MOSES, the University of Wisconsin Press, (Madison, Milwaukee, and London), 1968. Some of the other African-Americans who led Africans "BACK TO AFRICA" were the following: Chief Sam, Captain Martin Delaney, Dr. Edward Wilmot Blyden, Rev. Henry Highland Garnett, and Mother Mary Sankha - all of these during the 18th and 19th century C.E. Some of them actually commanded sailing ships that physically returned African brothers and sisters to the PROMISELAND - "Mother Africa" - ALKEBU-LAN.

46. Those who love their "Negroes" more than "Negroes" love themselves opposed the attempt of BLACKS' return to their own "Promiseland" - Mother Africa; but failed to oppose DeValera's return to free the Irish from the British; Wise's BACK TO ISRAEL (Zionism); even Castro's return to free Cuba from Batista. "Negroes" are the only "Americans"??? who are expected to have no other alternative for freedom than WHITE-prescribed "Integration" or "Amalgamation," neither of the latter two (WHITE-AMERICANS) can tolerate - Martin Luther King, Jr's death being the latest fatal proof. Like Crispus Attucks in the War of (White Peoples) Independence, King also died to protect a White America which do not intend to have a FREE AFRICAN PEOPLE - its former SLAVE CHILDREN being no exception.

47. The year the Right Rev. Bishop Bartolome de LasCasas of Spain (on the Island of Hispaniola, Spanish West Indies) initiated the bestial AFRICAN SLAVE TRADE of Moors from Spain, followed by Africans from the mainland (Africa) in 1506 C.E.; a SLAVERY that continues to this very day in the "Americas," and to much greater degree still in parts of Africa. This area of African people's experience needs no bibliographical reference, every Tom, Dick and Harry have already written on it, as if it was the only aspect of the "BLACK EXPERIENCE." See Eric Williams, DOCUMENTS OF WEST INDIAN HISTORY; Elizabeth Dannon, DOCUMENTS ILLUSTRATIVE OF THE HISTORY OF THE SLAVE TRADE TO AMERICA; Eric Williams, HISTORY OF THE WEST INDIES, FROM COLUMBUS TO CASTRO.

48. An African people brought to the Carolina Islands by their White Slave-masters, most of whom retained much of their cultural traditions from the Nigerian regions of West Africa, especially their language - "DIALECT." See Mason Crum, GULLAH NEGRO LIFE IN THE CAROLINE SEA ISLANDS, Duke University Press, 1940; Guy B. Johnson, FOLK CULTURE On St. Helena Island, South Carolina, Chapel Hill, N.C., 1930; PLANTATION NEGRO SAYINGS ON THE COAST OF SOUTH CAROLINA IN THEIR OWN VERNACULAR, Georgetown, 1899; Bennett, GULLAH: A NEGRO PATOIS; The South Atlantic Quarterly (Oct. 1908, Jan. 1909), G. G. Johnson, A SOCIAL HISTORY OF THE SEA ISLANDS, Chapel Hill, N.C., 1930; J. G. Williams, IS GULLAH A CORRUPTION OF ANGOLA?, Sunday News (Charleston, S.C.), Feb. 10, 1895.

49. Historically the term "JEW" identifies a member of the "TRIBE OF JUDAH." Using it in any other manner is incorrect. Since Whites no longer respond to the term "TRIBE," it is impossible to deal with them as such. The same type of rejection should be applied to "TRIVE" with regards to Africans. It is very similar to the term "GHETTO" which was applied for centuries to European and European-American (White) JEWISH Communities. Yet today in the United States of America the term is almost exclusively used in reference to "NEGROES" and "PUERTO RICANS."

50. Presently the FALASHAS, YEMENITES and COCHIMS provide the richest Hebrew groups in the State of Israel with respect to ancient Hebrew traditions in

terms of language, art, music and dance, religious carry-over, etc.; yet
they remain the POOREST financially, and are discriminated against by White
Jews because of their BLACK or BROWN color of skin. See the following for
further proof: Wolf Leslau, FALASHA ANTHOLOGY: The Black Jews of Ethiopia,
New York, 1951; J. M. Flad, A SHORT DESCRIPTION OF THE FALASHAS and KAMANTS
in ABYSSINIA, Chrishona, 1866; W. Leslau, THE BLACK JEWS OF ETHIOPIA,
Commentary, 7, 1949, pp. 216-224; H. A. Stern, WANDERINGS among THE
FALASHAS in ABYSSINIA, London, 1862; Y. ben-Jochannan, AFRICAN ORIGIN OF
THE MAJOR "WESTERN RELIGIONS," Alkebu-lan Books Associates, New York, 1970.

51. There are copies of Carletti's work in Italian and English in many
    libraries through-out the metropolitan New York City.

52. Judaeo-Christian Greek-Centric Anglo-Saxon imperialism, otherwise called
    "THE AMERICAN DREAM," "WESTERN CIVILIZATION," and/or "CAPITALIST
    DEMOCRACY."

BIBLIOGRAPHY OF WORKS USED BUT NOT CITED IN THIS CHAPTER

M. Grant, THE PASSING OF THE GREAT RACE, 1921

H.F.K. Gunther, THE RACIAL ELEMENT of EUROPEAN HISTORY, London, 1927

Basler, Rassen-und Gesellschaftsphysiologie, Berlin, 1925

L.S. Stoddard, THE RISING TIDE OF COLOUR against White World Supremacy, New York, 1920

Lynkeus, Der deutsche Buchhandel und das Judentum, Berlin, 1925

Belloc, THE JEWS, 1922

Burber, Die Judische Bewegung, 1916

W. Peters, Die Veverbung geistiger Eigenschaften und die psychische Konstitution, Berlin, 1925

M. Fishberg, THE JEWS, London, 1911

B. de LasCasas, HISTORIA de las INDIAS, Madrid, 1895

The Possible Improvement of the Human Breed, 1901 (reprinted in Essays in Eugenics, 1909)

G. Petzius, THE so-CALLED NORTH EUROPEAN RACE of MANKIND (in: Journal of Anthropology Institute, vol. XXXIX, 1909)

L.S. Stoddard, RACIAL REALITIES IN EUROPE, London, 1925

--------, THE REVOLT AGAINST CIVILIZATION, London, 1924

RACE MIXTURE WITH SOME REFERENCE TO BIBLE HISTORY (Victoria Sociology Journal, Vol. 67)

Heliodorus, ETHIOPIAN HISTORY (Underdowne, 1857, London, 1895)

WORKS OF LUCIEN (translated by W. Tooke, 1820)

Hertz, RACE AND CIVILIZATION, New York, 1928

R. Dixon, RACIAL HISTORY OF MAN, New York, 1923

G.M. Theal, ETHNOGRAPHY and CONDITIONS OF S. AFRICA BEFORE 1505, London, 1919

J. Blumenbach, ANTHROPOLOGICAL TREATISE, London, 1865

A. Churchward, ORIGIN AND EVOLUTION OF PRIMITIVE MAN, London, 1912

Quatrefages, THE PYGMIES, New York, 1925

J. Beddoe, COLOR AND RACE, (Huxley Memorial Lecture for 1924)

McCurdy, HUMAN ORIGINS, New York, 1924

W. Z. Ripley, THE RACES OF EUROPE, New York, 1923

R. Linton, THE STUDY OF MAN, New York, 1935

B. Wilder, PEDIGRE OF THE HUMAN RACE, New York, 1926

T. S. Forster, TRAVEL AND SETTLEMENTS OF EARLY MAN, London, 1929

Sorgi, THE MEDITERRANEAN RACE, New York, 1901

Pefrie, THE MAKING OF EGYPT, London, 1939

O. Bates, THE EASTERN LIBYANS, London, 1897, Vol. I

L. F. Barker, RACE HYGIENE AND HEREDITY (London & New York) 1924

Beddoe, THE RACES OF BRITAIN, 1885

Lundborg, RACIAL STRUCTURE OF THE FINNS OF THE NORTHERNMOST PART OF SWEDEN

Haddan, THE RACES OF MAN, 1924

Risley, THE PEOPLE OF INDIA, 1915

S. Lam Poole, SALADIN AND THE FALL OF THE KINGDOM OF JERUSALEM, 1898

Von Luschen, THE EARLY INHABITANTS OF WESTERN ASIA: (in Jour. Anthr., Vol. xli., 1911

F. A. Wright, FEMINISM IN GREEK LITERATURE..., 1923

Roper, ANCIENT EUGENICS, 1913

Vergil, AENEID, (date unknown)

F. Galton, HEREDITARY GENIUS, 1914

A. Weideman, RELIGION OF THE ANCIENT EGYPTIANS, London, 1897

E. Sandford, THE MEDITERRANEAN WORLD, London, 1934

F. Gillet, ANCIENT CITIES AND EMPIRES, Philadelphia, 1867

P. Sykes, HISTORY OF PERSIA, London, 1930, Vol. I

N. K. Duft, ARYANIZATION OF INDIA, Calcutta, 1925

R. C. Duff, ANCIENT INDIA, London, 1893

Thurston, CASTES AND TRIBES OF SOUTHERN INDIA, Madras, 1909

Elliott Smith, HUMAN HISTORY, London, 1954

Prince Liu-Nan, The Negritos de la Chine, Hanoi, 1928

Prof. Munro, PREHISTORIC JAPAN, Yokohama, 1911


C. Dover, HALF CASTE, London, 1937

E. A. W. Budge, LIFE AND EXPLOITS OF ALEXANDER THE GREAT, (transl. from the Ethiopic Texts), Vol. II, London, 1896

Gibbas, DECLINE AND FALL OF THE ROMAN EMPIRE, Dublin, 1781, Vol. I.

M. Fishberg, THE JEW, London, 1911

G. A. Massey, BOOK OF THE BEGINNINGS, London, 1881, Vol. II.

Josephus, HISTORY OF THE JEWS ( Dissertation III ) London, 1841

74

J. Wheless, FORGERY IN CHRISTIANITY, New York, 1930

J. J. Williams, HEBREWISM OF WEST AFRICA, New York, 1930

Dermengham, LIFE OF MOHAMET, London, 1937

P. K. Hitti, HISTORY OF THE ARABS, London, 1937

C. Dawson, THE MAKING OF EUROPE, New York, 1932

Le Jardin Parfume Nefzawi, HISTORY OF THE NEGRO, Doreramus, Paris, 1927

Ladolphus, HISTORY OF ETHIOPIA, London, 1682

J. A. Rogers, 100 AMAZING FACTS ABOUT THE NEGRO, New York, 1926 (pamphlet)

L. Froebenius, VOICE OF AFRICA, London, 1910-12

W. B. Harris, YEMEN, Edinburgh, 1843

W. Muir, LIFE OF MOHAMET, London, 1894

W. Armisted, A TRIBUTE TO THE NEGRO, London, 1840

Vicuna, Historia de Espana (date unknown)

ITALY, SPAIN AND PORTUGAL, New York, 1845

J. C. Murphy, TRAVELS IN PORTUGAL IN 1789-90

H. B. Cotterill, FROM DANTE TO FASSO, New York, 1919

Ruvigny, THE TITLED NOBILITY OF EUROPE, London, 1914

Burke's, PEERAGE, London, 1936

W. W. Brown, THE RISING SON, 1874

Shufeldt, THE NEGRO: MENACE TO AMERICAN CIVILIZATION, New York, 1907

Sir G. Higgins, ANACALYPSIS, London, 1897 (1927), 2 Vols.

D. Wilson, ARCHAEOLOGY OF SCOTLAND, Edinburgh, 1851

R. W. Bain, GUSTAVE III, London, 1894, Vol. I

McRitchie, ANCIENT AND MODERN BRITAINS, London, 1884, Vol. II

T. Fuller, WORTHIES OF ENGLAND, London, 1840, Vol., II

D. K. Hill, CATALOGUE OF CLASSICAL BRONZE SCULPTURE IN THE WALTERS ART GALLERY, Baltimore, 1949

G. M. A. Hanfmann, CLASSICAL SCULPTURE, Greenwich, Conn., 1967

ART TREASURES OF TURKEY (Smithsonian Institute, 1966-1968, Wash. D.C., 1966)

H. B. Walters, SELECT BRONZES, GREEK, ROMAN, AND ETRUSCAN, IN THE DEPARTMENT OF ANTIQUES, (British Museum), London, 1915

H. R. Hall, THE ANCIENT HISTORY OF THE FAR EAST, London, 1913

J. Soames Nickerson, A SHORT HISTORY OF NORTH AFRICA, New York, 1961

H. E. Barnes, AN INTELLECTUAL AND CULTURAL HISTORY OF THE WESTERN WORLD, New York, 1937, 3 vols.

------, THE CAMBRIDGE ANCIENT HISTORY, London, 1930, 9 vols.

I. Asimon, THE NEAR EAST, Boston, 1968

R. Grams and R. Patal, HEBREW MYTHS, New York, 1963

J. Lindsay, THE ANCIENT WORLD, New York, 1968

-------, CAMBRIDGE ANCIENT HISTORY, New York, 1924, vol's 1 & 2

W. A. Waddell, THE MAKERS OF HISTORY, New Delhi, 1968

W. Howells, MANKIND IN THE MAKING, New York, 1959

A. Montagu, MAN'S MOST DANGEROUS MYTH, THE FALLACY OF RACE, New York, 1964

S. Cole, PREHISTORY OF EAST AFRICA, New York, 1963

L. Cotlow, IN SEARCH OF THE PRIMITIVE, Boston, 1942

G. Childs, THE MOST ANCIENT EAST, New York, 1928

C. W. Ceram, The Secret of the HITTITES, New York, 1970

-----, RACE QUESTION IN MODERN SCIENCE (U.N.E.S.C.O.), New York, 1956

-----, ENCYCLOPEDIA OF RELIGION AND ETHICS, New York, 13 vols.

G. G. M. James, STOLEN LEGACY, New York, 1954

F. Thilly, HISTORY OF PHILOSOPHY, New York, 1914

A. Weber, HISTORY OF PHILOSOPHY (transl. by F. Thilly), New York, 1928

Dr. J. E. Erdmann, HISTORY OF PHILOSOPHY, London, 1893, 3 vols.

E. Sandford, THE MEDITERRANEAN WORLD IN ANCIENT TIMES, New York, 1938

J. J. I. Dollinger, GENTILE AND THE JEW (transl. by N. Darnell), London, 1862, 2 vols.

A. Eban, MY PEOPLE: THE STORY OF THE JEWS, New York, 1968

----, THE HISTORIES OF POLYBUS (transl. from the text of F. Haltseh by Evelyn S. Shickburgh) Indiana, 1962, 2 vols.

B. Mertz, TEMPLES, TOMBS AND HIEROGLYPHS; THE STORY OF EGYPTOLOGY, New York, 1964

J. B. Pritchard (ed.), THE ANCIENT NEAR EAST, Princeton, 1958

E. H. Blakeney (ed.), THE HISTORIES OF HERODOTUS, (transl. by G. Rawlinson), London, 1910, 2 vols.

H. R. Trevor-Roper (gen'l. ed.), HERODOTUS: HISTORY OF THE GREEK AND PERSIAN WAR (transl. by G. Rawlinson/Edited and Abridged with an introduction by W. G. Forrest), New York, 1963

M. Komroff (ed.), THE HISTORY OF HERODOTUS, (transl. by G. Rawlinson), New York, 1956

A. De Buck & A. H. Gardiner (ed.), THE EGYPTIAN COFFIN TEXTS, Univ. of Chicago, Ill., 1923 (gen'l editor James H. Breasted), 4 vols.

S. A. B. Mercer, LITERARY CRITICISM OF THE PYRAMID TEXTS, London, 1956

E. O. James, THE ANCIENT GODS: THE HISTORY AND DIFFUSION OF RELIGION IN THE ANCIENT NEAR EAST AND THE EASTERN MEDITERRANEAN, New York, 1960

T. W. Doane, BIBLE MYTHS AND THEIR PARALLELS IN OTHER RELIGIONS, Boston, 1882

T. Gaster, MYTH, LEGEND, AND CUSTOM IN THE OLD TESTAMENT, New York, 1969

Sir J. Frazer, FOLKLORE IN THE OLD TESTAMENT, London, 1918, 3 vols.

Drioton, Contenau and Duchensne-Guillemin, RELIGIONS OF THE ANCIENT EAST, (transl. by M. B. Loraine from the French), New York, 1959

I. Mayer, QABALLAH, Philadelphia, 1888

R. Oliver and G. Mathew (ed.), HISTORY OF EAST AFRICA, London, 1963, 2 vols.

G. Maspero, THE DAWN OF CIVILIZATION, (ed. by A. H. Sayle and transl. by M. L. McClure), London, 1896, 3 vols.

B. H. Warmington, CARTHAGE, New York, 1960

J. Lindsay, DAILY LIFE IN ROMAN EGYPT, London, 1963

C. Aldred, THE EGYPTIANS, New York, 1961

S. R. K. Glanville (ed.), THE LEGACY OF EGYPT, London, 1942

W. B. Emery, EGYPT IN NUBIA, London, 1965

J. H. Breasted, A HISTORY OF EGYPT, New York, 1909

M. A. Murray, THE SPLENDOR THAT WAS EGYPT: A GENERAL SURVEY OF EGYPTIAN CULTURE AND CIVILIZATION, New York, 1969

P. Montet, ETERNAL EGYPT, New York, (transl. from the French by D. Weightman), New York, 19

G. Steindorff and K. C. Seele, WHEN EGYPT RULED THE EAST, Chicago, 1942

J. A. Wilson, THE BURDEN OF EGYPT: AN INTERPRETATION OF ANCIENT EGYPTIAN CULTURE, Chicago, 1951

E. R. Bevan, THE HOUSE OF PTOLEMY, Chicago, 1927

J. H. Breasted, ANCIENT RECORDS OF EGYPT, Univ. of Chicago, Ill., 1906

J. Hawkes and Sir L. Wooley, PREHISTORY AND THE BEGINNINGS OF CIVILIZATION, New York, 1963, 2 vols.

N. Nesturkh, THE ORIGIN OF MAN (transl. from the Russian by the late G. H. Hanna), Moscow, U.S.S.R., 1959

The following pages introduce, for the first time, one of the outstanding African-Caribbean historian's work in the area of "BLACK STUDIES" and "AFRICAN STUDIES" in the United States of America. George E. Simmonds for the past few years has been teaching at the Harlem Preparatory School of New York, Inc., New York City, where he head's the "African, African-American and African-Caribbean Studies Department." An associate of very long standing, Mr. Simmonds, now finally finds time to record just a tiny morsel of the "mental food" he feeds his students at "Harlem Prep." It is the same kind of "food" he fed those students he taught two Summers ago at Gannon College, Erie, Pennsylvania. "FOOD" which caused the ERIE DAILY TIMES of July 8, 1970 to publish the following about his mental dietary skills:

> "IT IS EASY TO SEE WHY GEORGE SIMMONDS USES HIS
> SUBJECT TO INSPIRE."

One of the citations that brought forward the above comment by Sister M. L. Kownacki, the author of the article in the newspaper, was the following by Mr. Simmonds:

> "I WANT TO REPLACE EGYPT IN THE CONTINENT OF AFRICA
> AND PROVE THAT THE ANCIENT EGYPTIANS WERE NOT
> CAUCASIANS."

## "THINGS" DONE BY AFRICA
## BEFORE EUROPE

In this article the author will very briefly show some of the many "THINGS" the continent of Africa has given to the world before the coming of Europe into history.

It is taken from the writer's much more extensive work "AFRICANS INFLUENCE ON EUROPEANS FEAR OF HISTORY," presently being edited for publication. The larger work shows the reasons why TRUE HISTORY has been suppressed and kept from the peoples of the world.

Because of the old myths and teachings that "AFRICA (Alkebu-lan) HAS NO HISTORY" this article is written from a point to that perspective. The reader, in this context, can then see many reasons for the terrible fear of African History being taught truthfully in a white (European)-oriented society or setting.

One needs to remember, especially if one happens to be living in the United States of America, that it was, and still is, important to make the black man feel and see himself as INFERIOR to those Whites who dominate him. In the United States of America there is a very large population of black people, way in excess of what one can fine anywhere in all of Europe. This means that no single European country has anything nearly as close to the United States of America's black population living within its boundary. However, although the Europeans were, and in many instances still remain, conquerors and colonizers of the black man, their internal domestic relationship with him is slightly different than it is in the United States of America.

In order to control the numerous former chattel slaves, it was (from a white-European perspective) necessary to keep the black man totally ignorant of his "Motherland" - AFRICA; and make him psychologically ashamed of himself and the color of his skin. Such controls make blacks think that they ought to

be grateful and thankful to the whites for "discovering" (a term Europeans
love to use whenever they first find out that something, someone, or some
place existed of which they knew nothing) them in "backward Africa" and taking
them to "stolen lands" in what is commonly referred to in history and other
disciplines as the "New World" (the Americas - both North and South, and the
Caribbean Islands).

Since everyone (allegedly) knows that people of European descendants are
the only ones "civilized" and "Christianized",[1] we shall call upon the records
of history to present facts to the contrary in the forefront and to the
attention of what we today, hope is a newly enlightened world.

Let us begin to reopen the pages of history and examine some of the many
"THINGS" given to the world by Africans while many of those who have made
claims to be "the world's civilizers and protectors" were not yet in history;
and even their ancestors were not yet "civilized."

THE BIRTH OF MAN OR MAN-LIKE CREATURES:

First, let us begin from the birth of man or man-like creatures from a
non-religious, but scientific position. It is a very well established fact by
now among the "world's greatest authorities" that man left from Africa and
populated the rest of the habitable portion of the planet EARTH.[2] And, no
where else on EARTH has man been able to find any "fossil-man" half as old as
Zinjanthropus boisie that was unearthed by Dr. Louis S. B. Leakey and his wife
Mary in the Olduvai Gorge of Tanganyika (Tanzania), East Africa on July 17,
1959.

Zinjanthropus boisie is scientifically dated to be approximately 1,750,000
years old; meanwhile the oldest of the fossil-remains found in Asia (as of this
writing), commonly called "Java" and "Peking" man (found in remotely different
parts of the continent of Asia), are more or less the same age - approximately
500,000 years old. The latter two are classified anthropologically as
Pithecanthropi (singular, Pithecanthropus). The anthropological distinction
between both finds are: Java man - "Pithecanthropus Erectus", and the Peking
man - "Sinanthropus." As for Europe, its oldest find so far is called "Heidelberg man." It was discovered in the Mauer sands near Heidelberg (the origin of

80

its name), and is dated to be from the first Gunz Mindel interglacial phase.[3] This places him to be probably as old as 500,000 years - the key word to observe here is "probably." One can now see that man existed in Africa thousands, and most likely millions, of years before he did in the rest of the world; at least according to the latest evidence archaeologically and anthropologically.

Since Dr. Louis S. B. Leakey's finding of Zinjanthropus boisie, there have been other datings of man-like creatures found in East Africa. Findings have taken place in such countries as Ethiopia, one dated by the University of Chicago to be c4,000,000 years old; and in Kenya, one dated by Harvard University to be c5,500,000 years old. These two finds were published in the New York Times, the first one on May 1, 1969; the latter on February 19, 1971.

Here we are able to see AFRICA as the "mother of mankind" and "Queen of the earth." Not only did AFRICA give birth to the human family, she also gave to the world an over abundance of natural resources unmatched elsewhere.

Secondly: AFRICA gave the sons who "NAMED THE HEAVENLY BODIES. Great African astrologers also "NAMED THE SUN, MOON, STARS, and PLANETS..." says Lucian (one of Europe's "greatest" ancient writers). Thus, Count C. F. Volney of France in 1791 wrote in his book, THE RUINS:

> "There a people, now forgotten, discovered, while others
> were yet barbarians, the elements of the arts and sciences.
> A race of men now rejected from society for their sable
> skin and frizzled hair, founded on the study of the laws
> of nature, those civil and religious systems which still
> govern the universe."[4]

All of these "THINGS" the Africans accomplished while the Europeans (Volneys ancestors) and others were yet "barbarians." But we are not taught any of these "THINGS" in school; it is always the reverse (or opposite) according to our instructors of today, in order to maintain the same old stereotype myths and teachings of "the black man's racial and cultural inferiority to the white man."

THE BUILDERS OF THE GREAT PYRAMIDS OF EGYPT WERE BLACK MEN:

The Africans, called "EGYPTIANS" by Herodotus (whom Europeans refer to as the "Father of History"), had "...black skin and woolly hair...," and are the people in which reference is now being made. Reference is not being made about the Egyptian as he is today, the result of the many conquests he suffered by foreign invaders from Asia and Europe (B.C. to A.D.). Reference is to his original "black skin" and "woolly hair," and to his ancestors who were the builders of the major pyramids of ancient Egypt. Such lovely edifice as the Great (or Grand) Step Pyramid of Sakhara (Saqqara) was built during the Old Kingdom period of the IIIrd Egyptian Dynasty (between c2980 B.C.E. and c2700 B.C.E., depending upon one's chronology) during the reign of Pharaoh (King) Djoser (Zoser); built by the "great builder," Imhotep (who is referred to later on as "the world's first and oldest Stone architect).

The other three Great Pyramids of Egypt were built on orders of other Pharaohs. The first by Pharaoh Khufu ("Cheops") according to the Greeks who could not pronounce his name"; the second by Pharaoh Khafra (Chephren); and the third by Pharaoh Mkarere (Mycerinus). None of these massive pyramids was built after the IV[th] Dynasty, which was long before the arrival of the first so-called Semites or Caucasians on the stage of world history. This also preceded the "people of the bible" - the Hebrews (Jews); including the individual ascribed to being the first Hebrew who was Abraham (Abram, Ibrahim; all of these names having been given the same person).[5]

THE PYRAMID TEXTS:

Religious writings that can be found, even today, in the pyramids and other monuments of Egypt where many of the present biblical teachings, sayings and scriptures that are now ascribed to famous Hebrew prophets and other personages such as Job, Jeremiah and King Solomon (even that which is known as the "Proverbs")[6] had their origin in the Pyramid Texts.

THE COFFIN TEXTS:

Religious writings and symbols the Egyptians placed inside the coffin of their dead; and like the Pyramid Texts, they too have been co-opted as Jewish and Christian biblical sayings and scriptures by "God-inspired" writers (personalities).

Collectively these two works, the Pyramid Texts and Coffin Texts, form the major foundation for another ancient masterpiece known to us as the "Egyptian BOOK OF THE DEAD" (including the PAPYRUS OF ANI) - rightfully referred to by the ancients as the "BOOK OF THE COMING FORTH BY DAY." This is the book which most theologians would not like to become too well known; as it will expose much of their ignorance about the very profession of which they are supposed to be the "AUTHORITY." Within the BOOK OF THE DEAD is found stories of <u>Saviours</u> and <u>Resurrections</u> before the birth of Jesus Christ. Also, one can find <u>Virgin Births</u> taking place before the arrival or appearance of Jesus Christ, or his mother - Mary, on the world scene. (See picture of an Egyptian <u>"Virgin Mother and Child"</u> (Black Madonna and Child) on page 85 of this work.

THE "GREATEST AND EARLIEST" STONE ARCHITECT:

The world's greatest pyramid builder ever known was <u>Imhotep.</u> He was also the Grand Vizier to Pharaoh Djoser (Zoser); and as his personal architect, was given the task of designing and building Djozer's own pyramid (tomb) - c3000 or c2875 B.C.E.* Imhotep, then, proceeded to build what is today "ONE OF THE "WONDERS OF THE WORLD." His name, IMHOTEP, became a legend among later genera-tions of Egyptians, who regarded him not only for his abilities as a builder and architect, but as a magician, philosopher, astronomer, and the <u>"father of medicine."</u> In the <u>Saite period</u> he was deified, and considered the <u>"Son of the (Egyptian) God - Ptah;"</u> while the Greeks identified him with their own <u>"God of Medicine"</u> - Askelpios.[7]

The massive <u>Step Pyramid</u> at Sakhara (Saqqara) built by Imhotep rose in six unequal stages to a height of 204 feet. The measurements at its base were approximately 411 feet from east to west, and 358 feet from north to south.[8]

THE WORLD'S OLDEST NAVAL POWER:

Ebypt's (Kham's) became a naval power about c2750 B.C.E. It was started by Pharaoh (King) Userkaf, and continued by his successor Pharaoh Sahure. It was first used when a fleet was dispatched against the Phoenicians on the coast of Phoenecia during the reign of Pharaoh Sahure. A relief was discovered in his pyramid temple at Abusir, which shows four of his ships with Phoenician captives among the Egyptian sailors. This is the earliest surviving representation of <u>Sea-going ships</u> (c2750 B.C.E.).[9] Another fleet was sent by Pharaoh Sahure to far away Punt (or Puanit; the name the Egyptians called the Somali Coast nation

*The original was by the African (Egyptian) High Priest Manetho during the reign of Pharaoh Ptolemy I (General Soter), which began on Alexander II ("the great") death - c327 or 329 B.C.E.

that was once located at the south end of the Red Sea, where the Gulf of A-den comes in contact with the Indian Ocean (Oceanus Indus).

PLANNED PARENTHOOD:

The earliest method of scientific birth control known in history was published (or recorded) by the Egyptians about c1550 B.C.E. This earliest Fertility Control Recipe is also called the "Ebers Papyrus;" Named for one Ebers who had absolutely nothing to do with its writing, just its current ownership.[10]

KINGS AND QUEENS IN EGYPT:

The beginning of the Egyptian Dynasties was about c3200 B.C.E., which is more than 2000 years before the coming of the Europeans on the scene of World History. This shows the Egyptians had lineage of Kings and Queens, as an organized function of their  system of government, long before the "civilizing of the Greeks" or the arrival of Europe from the backward ages.[11]

THE BUILDING OF THE GREAT SPHINX OF GHIZEH (Giza):

A statue of the greatest magnitude which is of a human head and a lion's body that represents the Pharaoh's power. It was built more than  1400 years before the reign of Thutmose IV (c1400 B.C.E.).

THE ONLY PERFECT GOVERNMENT RECORDED BY MAN:

This government occured in Egypt (Sais) around c2500 B.C.E. What is meant by a "perfect government"? One in which there was no bribery or corruption. To understand just what made this possible, is to understand the religious concepts and beliefs of the ancient Egyptians. At one time in Egypt (Sais), the Pharaohs were considered "Gods on earth." They were not considered the Images of Sons of God; but they were God - (Himself) in the flesh on Earth.[12] Here, again, one can see that in accordance with our present teachings about Jesus Christ being "the Holy son of God" (in the flesh), is what the ancient Egyptians (Black men) had already spoke of and represented themselves to be - God in the flesh on Earth. They did not have to wait until Jesus Christ was born and became another God in the flesh on Earth.

THE ANCH (ANKH).

This was the Egyptian Symbol the Greeks (Fathers of European civilization)

Obelisk of King Sesostris I at Heliopolis
Dynasty XII. Granite. Height approx. 66 ft.

Mother and child
Middle Kingdom. Bronze. Height 5 in.
Berlin-Charlottenburg, Staatliche Museen der Stiftung Preußischer Kulturbesitz, Egyptian Department

85

called "CRUX ANSATA." It is the oldest form of our present Christian Cross; meaning "LIFE." It is said that the very early European Initiates were introduced to this sign as the symbol for "THE GIVING OF LIFE." The following are only a few of the many variations of the Ankh (Anch): (*THE ORIGINAL ANKH).

This particular symbol should be known to everyone, especially the black man; for it was he who introduced it to the world, only to see it being returned to him in many forms of the present day Christian Cross (f-k). Now he is being asked to accept it as a "Christian symbol"; also, that it originated from Roman Christendom. But he, the black man, has been given no recognition whatsoever for its origin or creation in Africa. One can find the "Christian Cross" on the top of the many stolen Egyptian (African) obelisks re-erected in many places in Rome. In all of such cases the Roman Cross attached to them give the impression that the Obelisk was Roman built; also, that the Cross was placed there by the builders of the obelisks.[13] On page 85 there is a picture of one of the many Egyptian obelisk.

SCOTTISH RITES:

In Scottish Rites Freemasonry one swears to uphold Christianity, which is not the religious teachings of the Grand Lodge of Luxor that predated Christianity by thousands of years.[14]

The Secret Societies of the ancients were where the learned and educated ones could have been found. In these early Secret Societies the ancient Greeks (accredited as "the first of the civilized Europeans") went to study and to become "initiated into the world of knowledge and enlightenment".[15] An example of the very high regards that the modern whites (Caucasians or Europeans, depending on the environment or academic level one is dealing) have for the ancient Egyptians can be seen in a book written by Arkon Daraul in 1961, entitled, "A HISTORY OF SECRET SOCIETIES;" in which he wrote:

> "Almost anyone, for instance, can get away with telling anyone else that he was an Egyptian priest in a former incarnation: because there is so very little verifiable material available to prove the reverse."[16]

This also helps to show that many white writers are aware of the glorious past that once was Egypt, and are willing to accept and admit it. This due only to the fact that they see it as the history of Whites, "Semites" or "Caucasians," and not of blacks or "Negroes."

TRADES: "SON LIKE FATHER:"

The ancient Egyptians were practicing the manual trades long before the Greeks; all of which they did from the habit of the son following in the footsteps (or profession) of his father. Herodotus explained that "...the Egyptians were divided into seven classes..." named after their occupations: "priests, warriors, cowherds, swineherds, tradesmen, interpreters, and pilots." These different classes came from the various districts in which Egypt was divided. The military-class who was known as "Calasirians" and "Hermotybians," came from the following districts: The Hermotybians from the districts of Busiris, Sais, Chemmis, Papremis, the island of Prosopitis, and half of Natho. None of them touched trades of any kind; but all had a purely military education. The Calasirians were from the districts of Thebes, Bubasitis, Aphthis, Tanis, Mendes, Sebennytus, Athribis, Pharbeathus, Thmuis, Onuphis, Anysis, and Myecphoris. They, like the Hermotybians, were forbidden to follow any trade or craft, and instead received exclusive military training - "son following father."

Herodotus further stated, that he could not say with certainty, as to whether the Greeks got the custom from the Egyptians or not, like so much else. He also stated that the feeling was common that they did. Reference was made to the fact that other nations did the same as he observed them.[17]

In some places of Europe this custom still prevails as it does in many parts of Africa. This particular statement is important, because one can still hear remarks made that "the Africans are still primitive" because they practice son like father trades (professions). Nothing is said regarding different parts of Europe where they still maintain the "Son like-Father" tradition.

The Egyptians were the teachers of history to Herodotus ("Father of History" according to "modern" Europeans). The title "Father of History" is a very grave misnomer, unless someone really meant for it to read - Father of European History, since Herodotus himself wrote that he went to Egypt "to learn" the history of which he wrote; not only Egypt, but also of Greece.

The point in question here is; how old was the history recorded by Herodotus before the birth of Greek civilization? This being the case, then Herodotus could not be the "father of history;" but the recipient of it. True, he may be called "the father of European History;" but this writer doubts that he is even deserving of that title, because of other men, such as Solon - "the Law Giver" of Greece. Solon, who lived around c. 600 B.C.E. said that "Greece had no antiquity in History and no history of antiquity."[18]

We know that the Egyptian high priests were far better historians than anyone else of their time. This we know from the many writings that they left us on the walls of their tombs and monuments in Egypt and Nubia; also from the many papyri found and deciphered. Here, again, Africa is playing a major role in history before Europe, the same "Africa without a history;" Africa that "gave" or "donated nothing to the world or mankind" - according to 19th and 20th century white writers.

In brief, the following is a list of a few of the many other historical contributions that came to us from Africa before the birth of Europe in world history.

Egyptian Alphabet, Literature and Script. (See Prof. Hyma's, ANCIENT HISTORY, pp. 27-30).

The earliest known painting, (See James Breasted, A HISTORY OF EGYPT, p. 22).

Collection of Taxes (J. Breasted, ibid. p. 65).

Naming of the Gods (Herodotus, HISTORIES, Book II).

Naming of the Goddesses, Europeans (ibid.).

Making of Obelisks (See Henry H. Gorringe, EGYPTIANS OBELISKS).

Development of the Scribes (See Veronica Ions, EGYPTIAN MYTHOLOGY, p. 113).

Centers of Learning; where men such as, Moses of the Hebrew (Jewish) Bible got his beginnings. (Henry H. Gorringe, EGYPTIANS OBELISKS, p. 2).

Development of the Negative Confessions; where Moses got his Ten Commandments; (Sir E. A. Wallis Budge, OSIRIS, pp. 340-342);(Homer W. Smith, MAN & HIS GODS, p. 43).

Creation of many Religious (Holy) Trinities (ibid., p. 353).

The development of Bullfighting in Egypt early as the IV<sup>th</sup> Dynasty. (Huldine Beamish, CAVALIERS OF PORTUGAL, p. 7).

Introduction of the world's oldest known <u>Solar Calendar</u> of 365¼ days per year: about 4100 B.C.E. (James H. Breasted, A HISTORY OF EGYPT, p. 26).

These and many others are just some of the very many THINGS that came out of Africa before Europe. Emphasis on the above listed THINGS that came out of Africa before Europe. Emphasis on the above listed THINGS, plus many others, have been highlighted in the author's other work being prepared for publication.

Africa had and still has, a HISTORY; one that amazes mankind today because of all the fallacies that have been written and said about her. The author suggests that the reader continue seeking for the TRUTH and GREATNESS that once was Africa, and still is.

NOTES FOR CHAPTER II:

1. The teaching we received left most of us believing that "Europeans and their descendants" are the only ones that meet the criteria of being "civilized" and "Christianized". This is a misconception.

2. Jacquetta Hawkes, PREHISTORY, History of Mankind, p. 45, The New American Library, New York, 1963.

3. Jacquetta Hawkes, PREHISTORY, History of Mankind, p. 95, The New American Library, New York, 1963; See also, Robert Silverberg, THE MORNING OF MANKIND, Prehistoric Man in Europe, New York Graphic Society Publishers, Ltd., 1967.

4. C. F. Volney RUINS OF EMPIRE, pp. 16-17.

5. Voltaire, THE PHILOSOPHY OF HISTORY, p. 69

6. Yosef ben-Jochannan, BLACK MAN OF THE NILE, p. 71; also "AFRICA: MOTHER OF WESTERN CIVILIZATION, p. 179; James Breasted, DAWN OF CONSCIENCE, p. 380

7. I. E. S. Edaards, THE PYRAMIDS OF EGYPT, p. 45; Yosef ben-Jochannan, BLACK MAN OF THE NILE, p. 109; J. A. Rogers, WORLD'S GREAT MEN OF COLOR, pp. 1-3

8. I. E. S. Edwards, THE PYRAMIDS OF EGYPT, p. 46

9. James H. Breasted, A HISTORY OF EGYPT, p. 127

10. Yosef ben-Jochannan, BLACK MAN OF THE NILE, p. 143

11. Hendrik Willem Van Loon, THE STORY OF MANKIND, p. 13

12. Mario Attilio Levi, POLITICAL POWER IN THE ANCIENT WORLD, p. 1

13. Henry H. Gooringe, EGYPTIAN OBELISKS, p.

14. This also holds true for York Rites Masons.

15. See Yosef ben-Jochannan, BLACK MAN OF THE NILE, chap. IX, pp. 187-204. Here one gets the opportunity to see where the many well known Greeks got their knowledge.

16. Arkon Daraul, A HISTORY OF SECRET SOCIETIES, p. 118

17. Herodotus, HISTORIES, p. 168

18. Note that Solon lived before Herodotus who traveled in Egypt c457-450 B.C.E.

BIBLIOGRAPHY:

Huldine Beamish, CAVALIERS OF PORTUGAL, Taplinger Publishing Co., New York, 1969

Yosef ben-Jochannan, BLACK MAN OF THE NILE, Alkebu-lan Books Assoc., New York, 1970

------------, AFRICA: MOTHER OF WESTERN CIVILIZATION, Alkebu-lan Books Assoc., New York, 1971

James H. Breasted, A HISTORY OF EGYPT, Charles Scribner's Sons, New York, 1905

Sir E. A. Wallis Budge, BOOK OF THE DEAD, Dover Publications Inc., 1961

-----, OSIRIS, University Books, New York, 1961

Arkon Daraul, A HISTORY OF SECRET SOCIETIES, The Citadel Press, New York, 1961

I. E. S. Edwards, THE PYRAMIDS OF EGYPT (date unknown)

Henry H. Gorringe, EGYPTIAN OBELISKS, Henry H. Gorringe, New York, 1882

Jacquetta Hawkes, PREHISTORIES, History of Mankind, The New American Library, New York, 1963

Herodotus, HISTORIES, Penguin Books, Baltimore, Maryland, 1968 (Translated by Aubrey de Selincourt)

Veronica Ions, EGYPTIAN MYTHOLOGY, Paul Hamlyn Publishing Group, Middlesex, 1968

Mario Attilio Levi, POLITICAL POWER IN THE ANCIENT WORLD, Weidenfeld and Nicolson, (English transl.), 1965

G. Maspero, NEW LIGHT ON ANCIENT EGYPT, T. Fisher Unwin, London, England, 1909

Pierre Montet, ETERNAL EGYPT, The New American Library, New York, 1964

Vagn Poulson, EGYPTIAN ART, New York Graphic Society Ltd., Conn. 1968 (English transl.), 1968

J. A. Rogers, WORLD'S GREAT MEN OF COLOR, Helga M. Rogers, New York, 1947

Robert Silverberg, THE MORNING OF MANKIND, New York Graphic Society Publishers, Ltd., 1967

C. F. Volney, RUINS OF EMPIRES, Truth Seeker Co., New York, 1950

Voltaire, THE PHILOSOPHY OF HISTORY, Philosophical Library, Inc., New York, 1965

BOOKS USED BUT NOT MENTIONED:

Robert Ardrey, AFRICAN GENESIS, Dell Publishing Co., Inc., New York, 1961

William Benton, EUCLID, - ARCHIMEDES, - APOLLONIUS OF PERGA, - NICOMACHUS,
      (THE GREAT BOOKS OF THE WESTERN WORLD) Vol. 11, Encyclopaedia
      Britannica, Inc., Chicago, 1952

      ------, PLUTARCH, (THE GREAT BOOKS OF THE WESTERN WORLD) Vol. 14,
      Encyclopaedia Britannica, Inc., Chicago, 1952

James H. Breasted, DEVELOPMENT OF RELIGION AND THOUGHT IN ANCIENT EGYPT,
      Harper & Row, New York, 1959

Prof. Lionel Casson, ANCIENT EGYPT, Time Inc., New York, 1965

Leonard Cottrell, THE LOST PHARAOHS, The Universal Library (Grosset & Dunlap),
      New York, 1963

Ignatius Donnelly, ATLANTIS, edited by Egerton Sykes, Gramercy Publishing Co.,
      New York, 1949

John W. Draper, THE INTELLECTUAL DEVELOPMENT OF EUROPE, Harper & Brothers,
      Publishers, U.S.A., 1903

Walter B. Emery, LOST LAND EMERGING, Charles Scribners Sons, New York, 1967

Sir James G. Frazer, THE GOLDEN BOUGH, The MacMillan Co., New York, 1967

Leslie Greener, HIGH DAM OVER NUBIA, The Viking Press, New York, 1962

      -------, THE DISCOVERY OF EGYPT, The Viking Press, New York, 1966

Jacquetta Hawkes, PHARAOHS OF EGYPT, American Heritage Publishing Co., 1965

John G. Jackson, INTRODUCTION TO AFRICAN CIVILIZATIONS, University Books,
      New York, 1970

Andrew Lang, MYTH, RITUAL AND RELIGION, AMS Press, New York, 1968

Emil Ludwig, THE NILE, The Viking Press, U.S.A., 1937

Bernard S. Myers, ART AND CIVILIZATION, McGraw-Hill Book Co., New York, 1957

F. W. Read, EGYPTIAN RELIGION AND ETHICS, Watts & Co., London, 1925

Robert Silverberg, LOST CITIES AND VANISHED CIVILIZATION, Chitton Co.,
      Philadelphia, 1962

Oskar Von Wertheimer, CLEOPATRA, George G. Harrap & Co., Ltd., London, 1931

Prof. Harold Orville Whitnall, THE DAWN OF MANKIND, Richard G. Badger Publisher,
      Boston, Mass., 1924

CONCLUSION

From the FIRST DAY in world-history BLACK (African or Ethiopian) people
all over the continent of Alkebu-lan (Africa) were denied their right of
recording their own LIFE-EXPERIENCES (style) as a direct result of foreign
conquests, imperialism and colonialism, and now neo-colonialism, from Asia and
Europe, then the United States of America, that very DAY the LAST "AUTHORITY
ON AFRICA" and her people (indigenous sons and daughters) ceased to exist.
This statement has no area of exception whatsoever. Neither does it cater to
any individual ACADEMICIAN, WHITE LIBERAL, CAUCASIAN, SEMITIC, or HAMITIC
"SCHOLAR." For Africa's TRUE EXPERIENCE can only be written by those who
EXPERIENCED it - BLACK PEOPLE, AFRICAN PEOPLE, NEGRO, OR ELSE (sons and
daughters of "Mother Alkebu-lan who the ancients called "ETHIOPIANS"); those
whose ancestors were described in the manner and characteristics used by
Herodotus, Polybius, Eusebius, Josephus  and others, all of which this work
has quite adequately detailed.

The REBIRTH of TRUE African History began in the year 1957 C.E. when the
Honourable Dr. Kwame Nkrumah, formerly Prime Minister and President of Ghana -
at this time in history degradingly called "BRITISH GOLD COAST CROWN COLONY
AND ASHANTE," led his fellow Africans of this glorious historic area of Alkebu-
lan's HIGH-CULTURES to become the first AFRICAN-CONTROLLED independent national
grouping and nation since the beginning of PARTITION in 1830 C.E. to the ending
of World War II in 1945 C.E.; taking her place at the side of the World's
oldest nation, Ethiopia, and Alkebu-lan's first republic, Liberia. At the VERY
NEXT DAY after said independence a FREE AFRICAN PEOPLE once again began to
RECORD AFRICAN EXPERIENCES (history) as seen through AFRICAN EYES; thus AFRICAN
AUTHORITY returned in "RIGHT" and "WRONG" as established through AFRICAN VALUE
SYSTEMS, and not from European, European-American, or "WHITE" Judaeo-Christian
Greek-Anglo-Saxon INTERPRETATION of what AFRICA WAS, IS, or WILL BE.

But, until African (BLACK) people are willing, and do write their own
HISTORY of their own experience, past and present, irrespective of what others
may feel or believe to the contrary, we will continue being SLAVES, mentally,
physically and spiritually, to Caucasian and Semitic RACISM and RELIGIOUS

BIGOTRY.

This short work, we know, follows no established "ACADEMIC SCHOLARSHIP" criteria by those persons or institutions we have cited with respect to the "SEMITIC-CAUCASIAN-HAMITIC" syndrome; neither of those who they represent. This is due to the fact that there could be no RIPPLE in the OCEAN if there is no RADICAL ERRUPTION of the SEA WATER; nor can there by any CORRECTION OF THE FALSE HISTORY PRESENTED OF AFRICA AND HER PEOPLE, Black People, if those WHO ARE GUILTY OF SAID CULTURAL AND PHYSICAL GENOCIDE are allowed to remain self-proclaimed "AUTHORITIES ON AFRICA" and of "AFRICAN PEOPLE."

We, as the authors of this work, have long-since before it became popular to realize that "...BLACK IS BEAUTIFUL...;" also realized that the need to RE-ESTABLISH that THICK and THIN lips, BROAD and NARROW nose, WOOLLY and STRAIGHT hair, BURNT and BLEACHED skin, people were indigenous to all shores along the banks of the Mediterranean Sea during the eras preceding the founding of Greecian High-Culture by Europeans, Africans and Asians (c. 600 B.C.E.), Etruscan High-Culture before that (c. 1000 B.C.E.), Hebrew or Jewish religious beginnings (c. 1630 B.C.E.), and even the so-called "First of the Semites" - Hyksos (c. 1675 B.C.E.), is our SACRED DUTY, irrespective of the PRICE TO PAY FOR SAME.

And, as this work reaches its final lines we, YOSEF ben-JOCHANNAN and GEORGE E. SIMMONDS, hold dearly to the following:

> HIS STORY (history) is as HE saw, heard, or read it.
> OUR STORY is the way we EXPERIENCED (lived) it.
> RIGHT-WRONG or WRONG-RIGHT depends upon ONE'S relation-
> ship to either position - HISTORY and/or OUR STORY.

NO ONE CAN TRULY WRITE ANOTHER'S HISTORY FROM THE OTHER'S PERSPECTIVE

Yosef ben-Jochannan
George E. Simmonds
September 1971 C.E.

OTHER WORKS BY THE AUTHOR

WE THE BLACK JEWS, Spain, 1949 (A Pamphlet in Spanish).

THE RAPE OF AFRICA AND THE CRISIS IN ANGOLA, Chana, 1958.

AN AFRICAN NATIONALIST VIEW OF BLACK POWER, New York CORE MAGAZINE (Winter
                Issue), 1966.

AFRICA: THE LAND, THE PEOPLE, THE CULTURE, (co-authors, Yosef ben-Jochannan,
                Ph.D., Kempton Webb, Ph.D., Hugh Brooks, Ph.D.), W. H.
                Sadlier, Co., New York, N. Y., 1969

SOUTHERN LANDS, (co-authors), W. H. Sadlier, Co. New York, N. Y., 1969.

SOUTHERN NEIGHBORS, (co-authors), W. H. Sadlier, Co., New York, N. Y., 1969

ARAB WORLD NEW AFRICA, (consultant to author), W. H. Sadlier, Co., New York,
                N. Y., 1968.

BLACK MAN OF THE NILE, Alkebu-lan Books Associates, New York, N. Y., 1970.

AFRICAN ORIGINS OF THE MAJOR "WESTERN RELIGIONS," Alkebu-lan Books Associates,
                New York, N. Y., 1970.

AFRICA: MOTHER OF "WESTERN CIVILIZATION," Alkebu-lan Books Associates, New
                York, N. Y., 1971.

African-American Heritage Series Publications
    (currently being edited for future release)
AFRICA AND HER EVER CHANGING MAP
ANOTHER ASPECT OF PAN-AFRICANISM
AFRICA (Alkebu-lan) IN HISTORY: A Chronology; 1,750,000 BCE - 1966 CE.;
                Seven Volumes.

OTHER WORKS BY YOSEF ben-JOCHANNAN:


WE THE BLACK JEWS, Spain, 1949 (A Pamphlet in Spanish).

THE RAPE OF AFRICA AND THE CRISIS IN ANGOLA, Ghana, 1958.

AN AFRICAN NATIONALIST VIEW OF BLACK POWER, New York CORE MAGAZINE
                    (Winter Issue), 1966.

AFRICA: THE LAND, THE PEOPLE, THE CULTURE, (co-authors, Yosef
                    ben-Jochannan, Ph.D.; Kempton Webb, Ph.D.;
                    Hugh Brooks, Ph.D.), W. H. Sadlier, Co., New York,
                    N.Y., 1969.

SOUTHERN LANDS, (co-authors), W. H. Sadlier, Co., New York, N.Y., 1969.

SOUTHERN NEIGHBORS, (co-authors), W. H. Sadlier, Co., New York, N.Y., 1969.

ARAB WORLD NEW AFRICA, (consultant to author), W. H. Sadlier, Co., New York,
                    N.Y., 1968.

BLACK MAN OF THE NILE, Alkebu-lan Books Associates, New York, N.Y., 1970.

AFRICAN ORIGINS OF THE MAJOR "WESTERN RELIGIONS," Alkebu-lan Books
                    Associates, New York, N.Y., 1970.

AFRICA: MOTHER OF "WESTERN CIVILIZATION," Alkebu-lan Books Associates,
                    New York, N.Y., 1971.

African-American Heritage Series Publications
    (currently being edited for future release)

AFRICA AND HER EVER CHANGING MAP

ANOTHER ASPECT OF PAN-AFRICANISM

AFRICA (Alkebu-lan) IN HISTORY: A Chronology; 1,750,000 B.C.E. - 1966 C.E.;
                    Seven Volumes.


96

# Titles by Yosef ben-Jochannan
# Available from Black Classic Press

## Africa Mother of Western Civilization

Dr. Ben examines the African foundations of Western civilization. In lecture/essay format, he identifies and corrects myths about the inferiority and primitiveness of the indigenous African people and their descendants. He mentions many authorities on Africa and their works, and proves how they are racist in intent.
ISBN 0-933121-25-3. 1971*, 1988. 750 pp. illus. Paper. $34.95.

## Black Man of the Nile

In a masterful and unique manner, Dr. Ben uses *Black Man of the Nile* to challenge and expose "Europeanized" African history. He reveals distortion after distortion made in the long record of African contributions to world civilization. Once these distortions are exposed, he attacks them with a vengeance, and provides a spellbinding corrective lesson.
ISBN 0-933121-26-1. 1972*, 1989. 381 pp. illus. Paper. $29.95.

## A Chronology of the Bible:
## Challenge to the Standard Version

Chronology documents the African origins of Judaism, Christianity, and Islam. Dr. Ben traces some of the significant influences, developments, and people that have shaped and provided the foundation for the holy books used in these religions.
ISBN 0-933121-28-8. 1972*, 1995. 24 pp. Paper. $4.00.

## Cultural Genocide in the
## Black and African Studies Curriculum

As Black and African studies programs emerged in the early 1970's, the question of who has the right and responsibility to determine course content and curriculum also emerged. In 1972, Dr. Ben's critique on this subject was published as *Cultural Genocide in the Black and African Studies Curriculum*. It has been republished several times since then and its topic has remained timely and unresolved.
ISBN 1-57478-022-0. 1972*, 2004. 150 pp. Paper. $14.95.

## Our Black Seminarians and
## Black Clergy Without a Black Theology

In *Black Seminarians,* Dr. Ben outlines sources of Black theology before Judaism, Christianity, and Islam and shows how their ideas, practices, and concepts were already old in Africa before Europe was born. Introduction by John Henrik Clarke.
ISBN 0-933121-62-8. 1978*, 1998. 109 pp. Paper. $14.95.

# We the Black Jews

Dr. Ben destroys the myth of a "white Jewish race" and the bigotry that has denied the existence of an African Jewish culture. He establishes the legitimacy of contemporary Black Jewish culture in Africa and the diaspora and predates its origin before ancient Nile Valley civilizations. This work provides insight and historical relevance to the current discussion of Jewish and Black cultural relationships.

ISBN 0-933121-40-7. 1983*, 1993. 408 pp. illus. Paper. $29.95.

# The Black Man's Religion
## Now available in three volumes

### African Origins of the Major Western Religions

In volume one, Dr. Ben critically examines the history, beliefs, and myths that are the foundation of Judaism, Christianity, and Islam. The Black Classic Press edition is a facsimile edition, with an added index and extended bibliography.

ISBN 0-933121-29-6. 1970*, 1991. 363 pp. Paper. $29.95.

### The Myth of Exodus and Genesis and the Exclusion of Their African Origins

In volume two, Dr. Ben highlights the often overlooked African influences and roots of the world's major religions.

ISBN 0-933121-76-8. 1974*, 2002. 74 pp. Paper. $14.95.

### The Need for a Black Bible

This third volume is an invaluable resource for anyone seeking to gain a better understanding of belief systems in the Western world.

ISBN 0-933121-58-X. 1974*, 2002. 120 pp. Paper. $16.95.

To order, send a check or money order to:

**Black Classic Press**
P.O. Box 13414
Baltimore, MD 21203-3414

Include $5 for shipping and handling, and $.50 for each additional book ordered. Credit card orders call: 1-800-476-8870
**For additional titles, please visit our website at www.blackclassic.com**

*Indicates first year published